Presenting the Past

Britain

Paul Grey
Rosemarie Little
Keith Worrall

Contents

All change: the Industrial Revolution

The empire on which the sun never set

Life in the middle class

The struggle for the vote

Published by Collins Educational
An imprint of HarperCollins*Publishers* Limited
77–85 Fulham Palace Road
Hammersmith
London
W6 8JB

www.**Collins**Education.com
On-line support for schools and colleges

Reprinted 2003.

ISBN 0 00 711459 1

British Library Cataloguing in Publication Data
A catalogue record for this publication is available
from the British Library.

Edited by Samantha Davey
Design by Ken Vail Graphic Design, Cambridge
Cover design by Derek Lee
Artwork by Peter Bull
Picture research by Sarah Clarke
Production by Jack Murphy
Printed and bound by Scotprint, Haddington
Cover image: The Peterloo Massacre, 1819,
          Manchester Central Library,
          Department of Libraries and Theatres

Britain is industrialised!

It's the start of a new century — look around you. Computers, machines, electricity, mass production and transport systems. These snapshots of Britain today show one thing very clearly — Britain is *industrialised*.

To be industrialised means several things. Most people live in towns or cities. They have homes with running water, gas and electricity. People work in factories, workshops or businesses. They send their goods or services by rail, road and air and communicate with their customers using the Internet, e-mail and fax. Without machines and without power our lives would be very different.

This book is not about Britain today, but the world we live in today does have its roots in the period we are going to study, 1750–1900. So much dramatic change took place in this period that we call it the **Industrial Revolution**. Revolution can mean 'big change'. In fact, there were several big changes between 1750 and 1900:

Farming improved and farming machines were invented which could perform tasks more quickly than people could. So, people left their villages and came to settle in the **growing towns**.

The **population** was growing. This increased the **demand** for **goods** such as food and clothing.

To meet demand, **inventors** made new **machines** to make goods faster and in greater number. **Businessmen** backed inventors by lending them money.

Money was used to build **factories** to produce these goods, using the new machines.

Better **transport** was needed to carry raw materials to the factories and to take the new goods from factories to markets. Money was invested to improve roads, dig canals and lay down railways.

Today, our industrialised society is the result of all these changes.

A Eurotunnel train at the entrance to the Channel Tunnel. Transport links improved during the Industrial Revolution because of the needs of industry.

A modern factory using computers. Factories were first built during the Industrial Revolution to house the bigger machines that could not be used in people's homes.

Water power and steam power were developed to work the new machines. These replaced human muscle power in certain industries. Electricity became a more important source of power in the period **after** 1900.

1 What does the word 'revolution' mean?

2 In what context do we use the word today?

3 Write a paragraph summarising the Industrial Revolution.

1750 ...

In 1750 most people in Britain lived, worked and died in the countryside. Subsistence farming (growing enough food for their own survival) was their main priority. The land was worked by muscle power – human and animal – and the seasons gave a pattern to rural life. In the summer, the corn was tended and harvested. In winter, there was less work to be done on the land. The few hours of light were used to make clothes and other necessities.

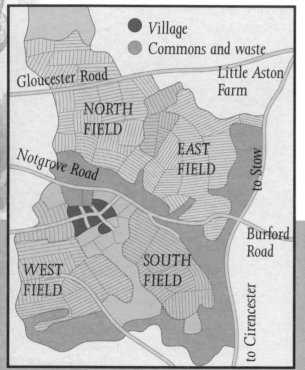

Village

Commons and waste

Gloucester Road

Little Aston Farm

NORTH FIELD

EAST FIELD

Notgrove Road

to Stow

Burford Road

WEST FIELD

SOUTH FIELD

to Cirencester

The village of Aston Blank, Gloucestershire, in 1752

Agriculture and **domestic industry** [producing goods in the home] went hand in hand. As soon as they were old enough, children were learning the customs of a way of life that hadn't changed for centuries. As long as people in rural areas produced enough food for themselves they saw no need to work harder or change their technology.

Changes over time can be shown through paintings, **statistics** [facts and figures] and maps. Below are some examples of the ways change can be studied. Look at what people did on farms in 1750 and then compare them with those on the opposite page.

Notice the land was farmed in strips. Farmers had strips in different parts of the village. All the villagers had a fair share of the land so that everybody had an interest in farming and how it was done. This was called the **Open Field system** because there were no hedges or walls to separate the strips of land. Between each villager's strip were banks [called **balks**] of unploughed land which kept them separate.

An early breed of sheep

These animals were reared mainly for wool. If you look carefully you can see the sheep is very thin. Compare its legs to those of sheep you can see in Britain today. When this animal was killed it wouldn't have provided many meals for its owner.

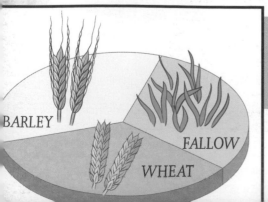

BARLEY

FALLOW

WHEAT

Farmers knew that they had to keep the soil fertile and that continual use drained the goodness out of it. The **fallow** year [when nothing was grown] allowed the soil to recover. Animals grazed on the fallow land and added valuable manure to help the soil regain its fertility.

The traditional method of crop rotation

6

... 1900

It would be wrong to suggest that all changes suddenly took place after 1750. Some were much more gradual and had started earlier, but by 1900, the amount of food produced by British farms had increased considerably. Production increased not because more people were working on the land, but because land was managed more efficiently and farming techniques had changed.

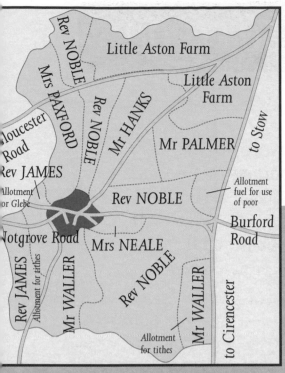

The village of Aston Blank, Gloucestershire, in 1850

Notice the way the land was enclosed in separate fields bordered by hedges. This happened to many farms in Britain because some new farming methods (such as the Norfolk four-year crop rotation) could only work if the open field system was replaced by separate fields. The separate fields were each owned or rented by one farmer. The new more efficient farming methods had to be introduced to feed the growing population. Enclosure Acts, passed by Parliament, allowed the larger landowners and tenant farmers to enclose the open fields, common land and wasteland.

From 1750 the population grew rapidly, which led to a big demand for meat. Robert Bakewell took two breeds of sheep and crossed them to produce the New Leicester sheep, which was good for meat as well as wool.

The New Leicester breed of sheep

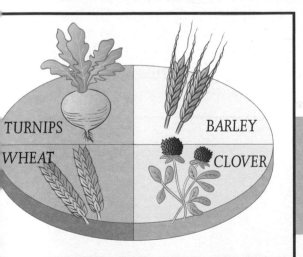

The most important feature of this system was that instead of leaving one third of the land fallow, all the fields were cultivated to produce more crops for food. Viscount 'Turnip' Townsend promoted the new method after using it on his estate at Raynham in Norfolk.

The Norfolk four-year crop rotation, developed in the early 1700s

1 What does the word 'subsistence' mean? In what context would you use the word today?

2 Make a list of the differences between the pictures from 1750 and those above.

3 Why do you think it would be necessary to increase food production if Britain was to industrialise?

Changes in transport: 1750–1900

1750 ...

In 1750 people and goods were transported by road, river or sea. Although many roads were in poor condition, important changes were starting to happen. One way the roads were improved was through Turnpike Trusts. These were groups of local people who wanted to set about improving their roads.

Parliament allowed the Turnpike Trusts to build toll gates on stretches of road and all road users had to pay a certain amount of money (known as a **toll**) to pass through the gate. This money was then spent on maintaining and improving the road. By 1770 turnpike roads covered 15,000 miles of England and Wales and, by 1821, the new roads considerably shortened journey times for stagecoaches from London. Wagons could carry twice as much as before on these better roads.

The journey time by stage coach from London to parts of Britain in 1750

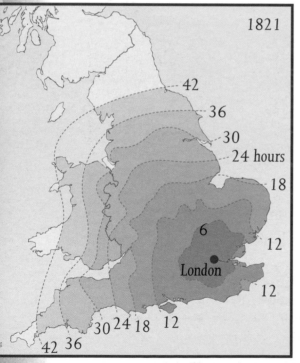

The journey time by stage coach from London to parts of Britain in 1821

Britain was lucky because it had long stretches of river that could be used for moving goods by boat. However, each river could only serve the limited area it flowed through and, as trade and industry developed, rivers could no longer carry the increased amount of traffic. Another solution was needed – canals. Canals were built from about 1750 onwards to carry goods.

Canals had an advantage over roads because bulky goods (like coal) could be carried in large quantities and relatively cheaply. The first canal was opened in 1757 to carry coal from the St Helens coalfield to the Mersey and the port of Liverpool, and to bring Cheshire salt to Lancashire. For the next sixty years, canals were the best form of transport for heavy goods. But, the railways were coming.

A canal barge loading coal from wagons on a horse drawn railway

... 1900

James Watt was one of the people who worked on developing a steam engine. Moving bulky goods on wheels on tracks using animal power was not new, but using a steam locomotive certainly was. The first locomotive was built by Richard Trevithick in 1804, and carried coal and iron in South Wales. **Colliery** [coal mine] owners around Darlington also wanted a cheaper and quicker way of transporting coal to the port of Stockton. Parliament granted them permission to build a railway, and they chose George Stephenson as the engineer. The 43 kilometre Stockton to Darlington line was completed in 1825. From then on, coalmine owners, industrialists and entrepreneurs saw the huge advantages of rail. Trains were fast and they could carry bulky goods and people. Railway **mania** [excitement] struck Britain in the 1840s. As you can see on the map below, Britain had a large system of railways by 1900.

The opening of the Stockton to Darlington railway, in 1825

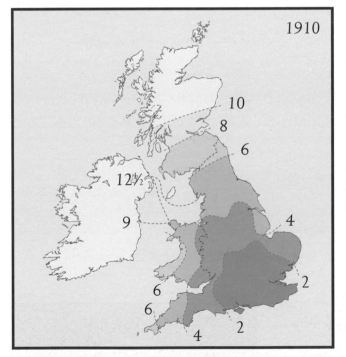

The travel time in hours by rail from London in 1910

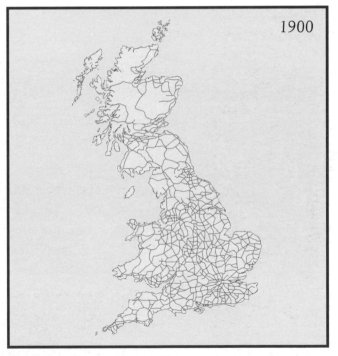

The railway network in 1900

1 Describe the changes in transport seen on these two pages. Overall, do you think they were good or bad for most people?

2 Looking at the information, what do you think would be the effects of an improved transport system on agriculture and industry?

3 Does the railway link your local area with other parts of the country? If so, find out when and why it was built, and how important it was to the development of the area.

1750 ...

In 1750 it did not make sense to divide *agriculture* [farming] from *industry* [making things]. Both were organised on a family basis. Parents and children would work on the land and at home, spinning wool or weaving cloth. This was called the Domestic System. People grew food to survive and made things to sell.

Between 1750 and 1900 dramatic changes replaced the domestic system. In its place grew an industrialised society with factories and large cities. The factory replaced the home as the place of work, water wheels and steam power replaced muscle power, and machines replaced hands. Look back at the chart on page 5 to remind yourself how the industrial methods replaced the domestic system.

Compare these industry pictures of Britain in 1750 with those on the opposite page in 1900.

Women and children would card the wool, which made all the fibres run in the same way. Spinning turned the fibres into thread. The thread was then woven into yarn. Long hours and low pay were common. Often the family would also have a small plot of land and perhaps a few animals. Children as young as four were involved in this Domestic System.

The domestic system in action: spinning wool in the home

Men usually did the weaving on a handloom because it required more strength. On Saturdays a clothier would buy the woollen cloth and take it to be **cropped** and **fulled** [processes that made the cloth thicker and improved the quality]. All of these processes did not take place under the same roof and did not produce enough wool to supply the growing population.

The domestic system in action: weaving cloth made from woollen yarn

... 1900

The switch from the domestic to the factory system was a gradual change during which large numbers of people left the rural areas to live and work in cities like Leeds. New factories meant new jobs. This was particularly attractive for those who had lost their source of income from the crumbling Domestic System. Many factory owners also provided new housing close to the factory for their workers. Of course, some stayed to earn a living from the land, but by 1900 only 8% of Britain's male labour force worked in farming, compared with about 40% in 1800.

What are the effects of working in mills and factories on children?

These machines could be easily operated by women and children. Youngsters were in great demand, their tiny fingers were ideal for tying together broken thread and they were small enough to squeeze in between the machines. Factory days were long – often fourteen hours.

Spinning machines powered by steam

Up to the age of 12 or 13, the bones are so soft that they will bend in any direction. This has affected the ankles and knees of many children who have to stand continuously for hours on end. Knees have become so weak that they turn inwards; this is called 'knock knees' and I have sometimes seen it so that the child has actually lost twelve inches of his height by it.

Cloth could be made faster and more cheaply than any one man could make. Low wages were driven even lower and the machines forced many out of work. New factories were built near sources of power like water and coal. With the canal and railway systems developing it was easier to bring in the raw wool or cotton and send the finished product out to market.

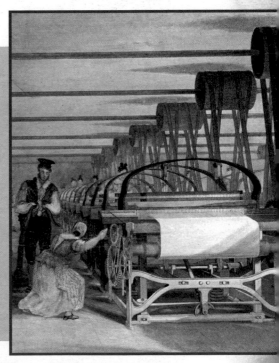

Weaving machines making cloth in far greater quantities than could be produced by the domestic system

1 Why did the factory system increase the quantity of wool and cloth produced?

2 Why did people go to work in the new factories?

3 Why were so many of the new factories built near rivers?

A revolution without railways?

Have you ever played the 'Supposing Game'? You have to use your imagination and knowledge to think about how the past might have been different, if certain events had never happened. Here, you and a partner have to work out what would have happened if railways had not developed during the Industrial Revolution. Would there have been a revolution at all? Or, would it just have happened more slowly and in a different way? Let's look at the effects of the railways.

1 Building railways needs lots of iron and steel. Lines, engines, wagons and carriages can't be built without metal! The railways created jobs in the coal, steel and iron industries, as well as construction (building the railways).

EFFECTS OF THE RAILWAY

2 Farmers benefited from the railways. Instead of walking cattle to market they could be sent by rail. Fresh foods such as milk could now be sent to be sold in the new industrial towns.

3 The railways could carry large quantities of goods more quickly than the canals or roads — and more cheaply. This helped industries and businesses to grow. Instead of selling just to local markets, manufacturers could sell their goods **nationwide** [all over the country]. People also had access to more goods.

The Supposing Game

1 If the railways had not been introduced in the 1830s what would have happened? Read the data in the **Fact File** opposite. Then, for each of the six **effects** of railways award a mark out of ten. Use these scores as a guide

◆ 10 = the Industrial Revolution would still have happened because roads, rivers and canals would have been used instead.

◆ 5 = the Industrial Revolution would partly have happened because roads, rivers and canals would have been used, but they would not have been so good.

◆ 0 = the Industrial Revolution would not have happened because roads, rivers and canals would not have had similar results.

4 *Canal companies and turnpike trusts lost money because of the competition from the railways. Workers lost their jobs.*

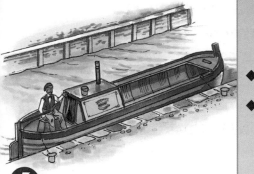

5 *Railway companies needed places to build and repair trains. Towns like Swindon grew around railway works. Towns like Crewe developed around railway junctions.*

WELCOME TO SWINDON

6 *Railways allowed people from all social classes to visit the seaside. Places like Blackpool and Brighton became large resorts.*

FACT FILE

Roads

◆ Roads were getting better from about 1750 onwards. More goods could be carried more quickly. Before roads were improved packhorses were widely used. The maximum weight each horse could carry was about 100 kilograms, whereas the same horse could pull up to 600 kilograms on wheels if the road surface was better. By the late 1830s there were 127,000 miles of road, although only 22,000 were in the hands of turnpike trusts.

◆ The cost of using the improved roads was high.

◆ In 1835 there were 14,000 regular wagon services each week in all parts of the country. Between 1851 and 1900 the amount of goods moved by rail increased from 60 million tons to 410 million tons, but the amount of goods carried by carts and wagons increased from 106 to 671 million tons.

◆ Journey times were faster on the new roads. In the 1750s it took ten days in summer and 12 in winter to reach Edinburgh from London. In 1836 it took just over 45 hours. This helped businesses because if a Londoner sent an order to Edinburgh in 1750, it would take about three weeks to receive the goods, but after 1836 it took just four days.

Canals

◆ At first canals reduced the cost of **carriage** [transportation] by at least half, and on the most efficient canals, by three-quarters. Between 1760 and 1830 over 3,000 miles of canals were built. This provided employment for thousands of men who then had money to buy the industrial goods.

◆ In the mid-1840s, canals carried more goods than rail. But, by 1898, canals only carried a tenth of what was transported by rail.

Look at your scores and try these activities:

1 List five impacts the railways would have had on each of the areas below. Which of these do you think would have been most affected:
a) jobs; b) leisure; c) transport?

2 Put the effects of the railways in rank order of the scores you have given them.

3 Overall if railways had not been developed, do you think the Industrial Revolution would have happened? Use this writing frame to help you:

The development of railways had several important effects, such as _____

Roads and canals did carry goods, but _____

However, railways did have some negative effects such as _____

If railways had not developed, I think the Industrial Revolution _____ happened, because _____. On balance _____

More and more people

One of the major factors that stimulated the changes in farming, industry and transport was the growth of Britain's population. The causes of this have been long debated. There is evidence that people began to eat a better diet and that medical treatment improved. Perhaps a more important cause was that people married earlier in their lives. In 1700 the average age of marriage was 27, in 1800 it was 20. In turn, this meant that couples had more children.

It wasn't just the population that increased. After 1800 Britain's cities grew as the population increased and more people wanted to live in cities rather than villages. When farmers started to use machinery instead of human labour, many of those who were out of work decided to try their luck in the cities. People needed somewhere to live, so new homes were built quickly to house them. These changes are closely tied to the other changes we have looked at in farming, industry and transport.

◆ More people need more food to eat otherwise there would be mass starvation. So, farmers enclosed their land and used new machines to increase food production.

◆ More people need more clothing to wear and goods to buy. The Industrial Revolution changed the way goods were produced so that the increased demands were met.

◆ The new factories (built to produce these goods) needed power and raw materials, so many factory owners sited their businesses near rivers or coal and iron ore fields. Housing was also built near the factories for the workers.

As a result of all of these changes, people were brought together in larger numbers than anyone had ever seen before. If 1750–1900 was the age of industry, it was also the age of the city.

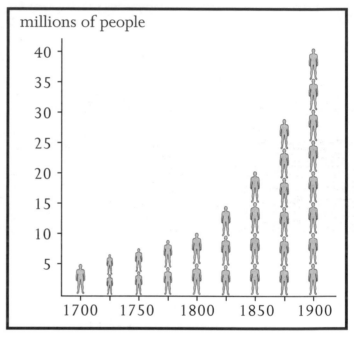

millions of people

The population growth in England, Wales and Scotland between 1700 and 1900

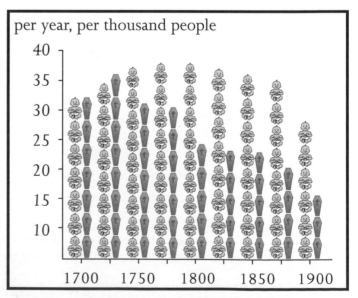

per year, per thousand people

The birth rate and death rate for England and Wales between 1700 and 1900

Leeds in 1715

Leeds in 1858

In 1843 parts of Leeds were described as "disgusting ... owing to a general lack of paving and draining, irregularity of building, the abundance of **courts** [courtyards] and blind alleys, as well as the almost total absence of ... cleanliness." This won't come as a surprise to you when you learn that the cities were not planned, that housing was poor as it was built in a hurry and that there were no rules about buildings and public health. In the early stages of the Industrial Revolution politicians did not believe in **legislating** [making laws] for social improvement.

1 Using the pictures and graphs explain how Leeds changed between about 1700 and 1900. Draw out a chart like the one below to help you.

Source	Description	Changes
Leeds in 1715		

2 Carry out some research in the library or on the internet to find out what historians suggest are the reasons for the increase in population. Remember to make notes on what you find.

3 In 1801 the first **census** [count] was taken and is now repeated every ten years. See if you can find out what the censuses in your area show about population changes during the 19th century.

The Industrial Revolution: causes and effects

As historians, you have so far looked at the changes that took place during the Industrial Revolution, but we haven't linked them to the causes or effects. Before we look at the causes and effects in more detail, the diagram below shows you how causes combined together to make the Revolution happen and what the effects were. These causes did not happen in sequence, one after another, but they acted together over time in a way that enabled industrialisation to take place.

THE CAUSES OF THE INDUSTRIAL REVOLUTION

What made the revolution possible?

- Large supplies of coal, iron-ore and metals like tin and lead.

- Long stretches of navigable rivers.

- Many natural harbours made coastal shipping possible.

- Britain's position on the north-western edge of Europe helped it to take advantage of trade around the world.

What made the revolution likely?

- Ambitious businessmen were willing to invest in new inventions and factories, and had the money to do so.

- Many ordinary people were willing to accept change.

- The changes in agriculture had already increased the production of food.

What triggered the revolution?

- New inventions improved production processes.

- New sources of power were used, for example, steam to power machines instead of human muscle.

- The population grew, which led to higher demands for food and goods.

- Better roads, the development of canals and then railways provided faster means of carrying goods.

Before

- Working on the land

- Small-scale production

- Using muscle power

- Selling to small local markets

THE EFFECTS OF THE INDUSTRIAL REVOLUTION

After

◆ **Working in factories**

◆ **Mass production**

Living conditions: Industrial cities developed rapidly on the coalfields. The speed of growth meant that the cities were overcrowded. They lacked clean water supplies and sewerage systems to take away waste. This led to poverty and squalor. After 1850, however, new laws did improve living conditions.

Communication and ideas: The new railway system meant that people, as well as goods, could travel long distances quickly. Trips to the seaside were possible, as was commuting. Newspapers, full of new ideas and current events, were printed in London and could be read all over the country the next day.

Protest and change: Living in closely packed areas and working in large factories prompted the working classes to organise themselves into groups to push for changes. Trade unions, for example, developed to protect workers in particular occupations or industries. Some of them fought for improvements in wages and working conditions, and others wanted a share of political power so they could make laws to make life better for the working classes. By 1900 the working classes had their own national political party – the Labour Party.

The economy: The economy grew and the country became richer. Britain became known as the 'Workshop of the World' because we made and sold goods to all corners of the world.

Class system: The middle classes increased in number because of the growing number of manufacturers, businessmen and professionals who had more money. There was also a growth in new jobs such as railway guards and shopkeepers. Meanwhile, the working class was left to deal with poor living and working conditions with no help from the government until later in the 19th century.

◆ **Using steam power**

◆ **Selling to national and international markets**

Growth of empire: Industrialisation required more and new materials which could be provided by Britain's colonies. The British Empire also provided markets where Britain's goods could be sold. As Britain grew richer the empire grew in size until it covered nearly one quarter of the world.

New machines and new power

One of the causes that made the Industrial Revolution happen when it did was the invention of new machines. These new machines not only mass produced things, but they did so much more quickly than any human could achieve by hand. The developments you can see on this page took place at the same time that demand for goods was growing because of the increasing population. What were the main inventions during this period and how did they change manufacturing processes?

Richard Arkwright

In 1769 Arkwright invented the water-frame. This machine was powered by water wheels and spun yarn that was strong. The 96-spindle water-frame was too big to fit into any home so factories had to be built. These were the world's first factories. By 1850 there were 2000 cotton factories producing far more cotton yarn than was possible in people's homes. The value of British cotton exports grew from £46,000 in 1751 to £5.4 million in 1800 and £46.8 million in 1861.

James Watt and Matthew Boulton

Many people tried to harness steam power to work machines. Watt and Boulton improved on the work of others and developed a working steam engine in 1775. Further adjustments to the design were made, and in 1785 the first textile mill took delivery of the steam engine which could run the new machines. By 1800 there were 1,200 of these in use. Soon the engine was adapted to act as a hammer in the process of making iron.

Eli Whitney

In 1793 in the USA, the cotton gin was invented by Eli Whitney. The gin machine made it far easier to separate the pod from the cotton – a process previously done by hand. This speeded up the production of raw cotton in the USA, much of which then ended up in British factories where it was spun into yarn and woven into cloth.

Richard Trevithick and George Stephenson

In 1804 Trevithick built the first locomotive, the 'Catch Me Who Can', which was powered by steam. But unfortunately, he couldn't convince others of the importance of his invention. George Stephenson improved on Trevithick's design in 1825 and opened the Stockton and Darlington Railway. His Locomotion Number 1 carried goods and people, and it made a profit. Soon other lines were built to connect towns, cities, factories and ports. With trains travelling at 30 miles per hour the new lines quickly linked factories to ports so goods could be sold abroad.

1 Draw out a table like the one below and decide what would be the good and bad points of each invention. Put your answer in your table.

Invention	good because	bad because
Water-frame	It produced cotton quickly and …	People who spun cotton at home couldn't compete and …

2 Which inventions are powered by **a)** water; **b)** steam; **c)** man power?

3 Do you think the Industrial Revolution would have happened without inventions?

Between 1550 and 1833 Britain was fully involved in the Slave Trade. Millions of black West Africans were forcibly taken from their homelands, shipped to North America and the Caribbean and put to work on plantations to grow tobacco, sugar and cotton.

Poor conditions on the slave ships led to many deaths during the voyage across the Atlantic Ocean and, on the plantations, brutal treatment cost the lives of many more. Slave traders made profits from the selling and buying of slaves and from what the slaves produced on the plantations. Merchants in ports like Liverpool, Bristol and Hull grew rich. But, to what extent did the profits from the slave trade help to finance the Industrial Revolution?

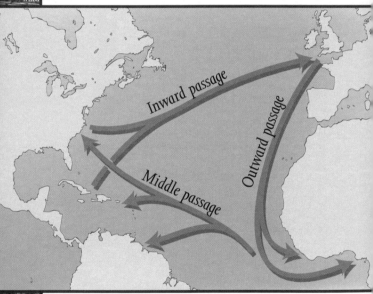

The routes of British ships during the Slave Trade or triangular trade

Inside a slave ship

❝My name is Eric Williams. In 1944 I wrote a book called *Capitalism and Slavery*. I think that the slave traders made enormous profits. The evidence suggests that traders made 30% profit – that means they earned a third more than they invested in the business. I believe that the profit from the Slave Trade was one of the main sources of money which financed the Industrial Revolution. This money made an enormous contribution to Britain's industrial development.❞

Industrial Revolution?

You Decide

Using the evidence on the following pages and what you have learnt about industrialisation, you are going to investigate the Slave Trade. You will decide if you agree with Eric Williams.

1 Did money from the Slave Trade help fund the Industrial Revolution? Look at each source and think about whether it could be used to support Eric Williams's argument.

Source 1 – Some of those who profited from the Slave Trade

'My name is Richard Pennant and I was an MP for Liverpool. I inherited 600 slaves and 8000 acres of good, fertile sugar plantations. I invested a lot of the money I made from my plantation and slaves in slate quarries in north Wales. Everybody knows that industrialisation only got going in north Wales after I invested my money from the Slave Trade.'

'My name is John Pinney. I came back to Britain from a career as a plantation owner in the West Indies. I am now worth £70,000. I have invested most of this in land, government stocks and shares. I did not invest any in industry or business.'

'I am Mr Fuller and I helped run my family's estates in Jamaica between 1734 and 1755. Back in Britain, we put a lot of money into charcoal ironworks and gun foundries in Sussex.'

Source 2 – Historian, Peter Fryer writing in 1993

The coal and iron industries of south Wales depended directly on the triangular trade for their initial funding. The north Wales slate industry was also financed by profits from the Slave Trade. The south Yorkshire iron industry; the Liverpool and Manchester Railway; the Great Western Railway; the original steam engine of James Watt: all were financed in part with profits from the Slave Trade.

2 Looking at the sources so far, do you agree with Williams and think that money from the Slave Trade helped to finance the Industrial Revolution? Use the table below to help you.

Evidence	Agree because...	Disagree because...

... Blood and profit: did slavery finance the Industrial Revolution?

When trying to make decisions about events in history, there are often different opinions to consider.

> **3** Look at the sources below and using the same table, decide whether you still agree with *Williams*.
>
> | Evidence | Agree because... | Disagree because... |
> | --- | --- | --- |
> | | | |

Source 3 Historian Kenneth Morgan, in 2000

Liverpudlians [people from Liverpool] invested in salt works, sugar refineries, breweries and in copper, glass and iron smelting in Liverpool and south Lancashire. Yet from surviving records it is impossible to establish what fraction of this investment came from overseas trade [such as the Slave Trade] rather than from other businesses.

Source 4 – Historian Kenneth Morgan, writing in 2000

The conclusions of recent research is that on average 'normal profits' of around 5% to 10% were achieved in the final years of the British Slave Trade: the view that the slave trade was a **bonanza** [source of wealth] is largely a myth.

> **4** After looking at these two sources, what is your opinion? Has it changed? If so, why?
>
> **5** It is often hard to decide what definitely happened in history, and the debate about the Slave Trade and the Industrial Revolution is still going on.
>
> ◆ Imagine this is the subject of a television debate between these two historians. Write a script for the debate they would have on television.
>
> ◆ You can chair the debate. What questions would you ask of each historian?
>
> ◆ Try to include in your script an outline of the debate, evidence for both views and your conclusion at the end of the programme.
>
> **6** Suppose the Slave Trade had not happened, do you think Britain would still have experienced an Industrial Revolution?

This is Olaudah Equiano. He was born in Nigeria in 1745, but was sold into slavery when he was a child. In 1797 he wrote his life story, *The Interesting Narrative of the Life of Olaudah Equiano.*

I had a very happy childhood. My parents had seven children and I was the youngest son. However, in 1756 when I was eleven all that changed. One day, when all the adults of the village were at work, three people climbed over our walls and stole me and my sister. They ran off with us into the woods. The next day was even worse than this - they separated me from my sister. I cried all the time and couldn't eat. I was so worried about what would happen to me.

Later that year, I was taken to a slave ship on the coast. I had never seen white men before and I was very scared of them. Worse than that though, were the conditions on the ship. There were many black people all chained together, and the smell was terrible. Because of the smell I could not eat and I was whipped severely as punishment. I did not know what my fate would be.

I was bought by a lieutenant in the British navy and, after travelling to Barbados and America, we arrived in Britain in 1757. My master treated me well, and I learnt a lot whilst on his ships with him. I was at sea for a long time fighting in the Seven Year's War. In 1759 while we were staying in England, I was baptised and stayed with a very nice family and even went to school. In 1762 we learnt that the war was over and I was overjoyed at the thought of freedom. Shortly afterwards, however, I received more bad news. Rather than freeing me, my master had sold me once again. I was distraught. At the beginning of 1763 I was taken to Montserrat in the Caribbean, and was sold to Mr Robert King, a quaker and a merchant. I was a slave again.

As it turned out, Mr King was a very nice man. He treated me better than I had known before, and let me travel on his merchant ship with his captain. As we were doing so well, in 1764 Mr King bought a bigger and better ship. Whilst on board the ship I tried my own hand at being a merchant. I did this for about four years and saved all the money I earned. My master promised that if I earned what he paid for me (£40), I could buy my freedom. In 1765 I found that I had £47. I went to Mr King and gave him the money. At last I was a free man. Eventually I returned to England where I married an English woman, and fought for the abolition of slavery.

1 Read about Olaudah's life. Using the living graph below, chart his feelings between 1745 and 1765, to show how they changed over time.

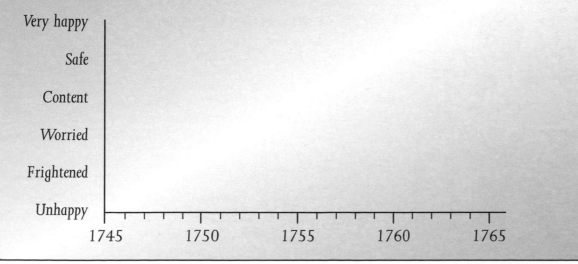

A royal visit to Leeds

This is Ellen and her husband Alfred. They have lived in Leeds all their lives. It is Monday 6 September, 1858, and Queen Victoria has arrived in Leeds to open the new Town Hall …

Alf! Alf! I've just seen the Queen! She arrived at the train station a little while ago and I was in the crowd.

Seems as if Leeds is finally being appreciated then? About time too. Last time we saw her was in 1835 when she was still the Princess, she came through Leeds on her way to somewhere more important.

Stop moaning! If we're lucky we might see her open the Town Hall tomorrow.

Oh, it's alright for her to visit the city when it's been cleaned up and given a lick of paint. But what about in the bad times? No king or queen came to see this city when it was struck by cholera in 1832. Thousands died but I never saw no crown then.

Well she's here now. And anyway things have changed. Take the factories. It used to be that no one in government cared about us little 'uns working long hours, bent double to piece together those bits of wool. At least it's better for today's kids — they get a chance to grow up a bit before they work.

Don't remind me, I still suffer with my back. Of course, there were thousands like us. Those wool mills sprung up like mushrooms after those big machines were invented. My Dad's little handloom was no match for them. He left his village and moved here along with others from the country. That's why I was born here in the city.

24

What was it like for your Dad when he first arrived?

To begin with it wasn't so bad. His wages in the factory were a bit better than the pittance he got for the cloth he wove by hand. But soon more and more mills sprung up. That was the start of the crowded, noisy Leeds you see today. Houses for the workers, all packed in tight, soon followed factories. No one had any privacy or any dignity. Of course, for the owners it was all different. They didn't want to live near their work or their workers. That's why their big houses aren't in the centre of Leeds but on the outskirts, in the suburbs like Hossforth.

Don't you think some things have got better? What about these new unions? Aren't they helping people like us?

In some places they are, but if workers can't read and write how are they ever going to get organised and fight back against the owners? Some, like those in the friendly societies are helping themselves, but others just used the hammer and flames to make their point. I pity those rioters who were caught. They got transported, locked up or worse. Anyway the unions won't help us, we're too old now. They're only interested in helping those of working age. Since I had to stop working last winter because of my back we're relying on our children for food and rent. Do you think the Queen thought of that when you saw her today?

*I suppose not, but it's still a great honour for the city. 1858 will be a memorable year. I wonder if she'll visit the new factories that spin **flax** [a type of thread]?*

I shouldn't think so. We know this city is about industry and nothing but industry, but the Mayor wants her to take back a different view of Leeds. She's only visiting for a few days — we've lived here most of our lives. Whose view of Leeds do you think she'll remember when she goes back to London?

1 Make a list of all the words in the text which are positive about the Industrial Revolution in one colour. Now, make a list of all the words which are negative about the revolution in another colour.

2 You are a wealthy businessman in 1858 who owns one of the flax factories in Leeds. Write a letter to the Queen thanking her for her visit, and explaining how the Industrial Revolution has changed things for you and how you feel about it. In your letter you should try to include the words below:

◆ Workers ◆ Railways ◆ Wealth ◆ Public health ◆ Steam-power ◆ Population

What was life like in an industrial town?

The new steam-powered machines could not be used at home – they were far too big. Factories had to be built to house them, usually near natural resources like water, coal and iron ore. Around these factories new industrial cities grew up as people flocked to find employment and higher wages. They found jobs but they also found living conditions that threatened the lives of adults and children.

Living in cities was a nightmare. Early industrial cities like Manchester, Leeds, and Sheffield became overcrowded. Thousands of people streamed in to the city from the country looking for work and soon found themselves living in back-to-back housing where noise, pollution, squalor and disease were common. Looking for a quick profit and with no laws to stop them, greedy builders put up about 70 back-to-back houses in an area the size of a football pitch. These dwellings had few windows, no clean water supply and only a cesspool for a toilet. In some parts of Manchester over 100 people shared one toilet. In environments like these it was no surprise that people's health suffered and epidemics happened regularly.

Diseases like cholera struck the city dwellers frequently. Between 1831 and 1854 four outbreaks occurred. Cholera was a major killer with sufferers experiencing diaorrhea, vomiting and dehydration. The germs that cause cholera live in the excrement of people who have caught the disease. There was no sewage disposal and at times waste was also thrown into the gutters in the streets. In London, for example, up to 200 sewers carried sewage straight into the River Thames. The water from the Thames was then used for cooking and drinking. Once the germs got into the drinking water cholera spread like wildfire through the cities.

At the time no one expected politicians in central or local government to do anything. Politicians didn't think they should interfere in people's lives. **Laissez faire** is the name we give to this attitude. Governments didn't interfere because this would be an attack on the freedom of the individual. At the time most people really believed that if government did intervene it would only make things worse.

Look carefully at the sources below. They will provide you with evidence of life in the industrial towns.

A letter from Edward Baines Jnr. to Lord John Russell, a member of the government in 1846. Baines believed in laissez-faire policies.

What are the duties of the government? Generally speaking, to maintain the frame of society. This means government should … make and administer laws needed for peace, order and justice.

It is not the duty of government to feed the people, to clothe them, to build houses for them, to direct their work … or to supply them with teachers, doctors, books and newspapers. These are things the people can and ought to do for themselves.

A

On the 26th May, 1832 the first case of cholera struck … and then spread very quickly. The disease has hit those parts of Leeds where there are no sewers, drainage or paving. In one area where 386 people live, there are only two toilets.

In one cul-de-sac in Leeds, called Boot and Shoe Yard, there are 34 houses and 340 people live in them. From this part of the city 70 cartloads of manure which had been untouched for years were removed. To build the largest number of houses in the smallest place seems to have been the original view of the builders. Thus, neighbourhoods have grown up in which there is neither water nor toilets.

Robert Baker, a doctor, on the state and condition of Leeds in 1842

The spread of back-to-back housing and deaths from cholera in Leeds in 1832

B Male life expectancy, in years, in two areas, in 1842. Rutland is a rural area.

	Rutland	Leeds
Professional classes Army officers, clergy, lawyers, business people	38	35
Tradesmen	41	27
Labourers	38	19

C

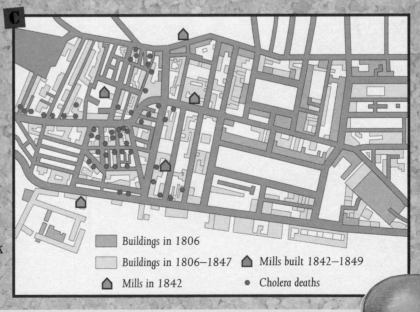

Buildings in 1806

Buildings in 1806–1847

Mills in 1842

Mills built 1842–1849

Cholera deaths

1 Using all the sources write a dialogue between these two people who lived at the time. One is a doctor. He has visited Boot and Shoe Yard and wants to improve conditions there, so that there are no more outbreaks of cholera. The other is an MP who believes in the laissez-faire approach of government. They are discussing the causes of and the remedies for the conditions in Boot and Shoe Yard.

What were working conditions like?

One important result of industrialisation was the building of factories to house the large machines that produced goods. At the start of the industrial revolution there were no laws about how factories should be run or about how employers should treat their workers. The people who worked in them were very much at the mercy of the owner. What were conditions like in these factories?

◆ Most factory owners were not bothered about the welfare of their workers. Many employed children because they could pay them less. Children could also squeeze themselves into tight spaces when machines broke down or when thread needed tying together. Boys and girls grew up with their backs twisted and deformed. Sometimes the children were cruelly treated.

◆ Another health hazard was the hot air. In textile factories it was important to keep the air humid and the temperature near to 30°C to prevent the cotton from breaking. Throats and lungs became prone to diseases in the absence of fresh air.

◆ Adult and child workers usually spent about 14 hours in the factories. Wages were low, particularly for women and children. During the 19th century however, reforms did make things better for factory workers, and owners could no longer do what they wanted. The Factory Acts of 1819 and 1833 shortened working hours for children, and further reforms followed in 1844 and 1847 which applied to women as well.

◆ Not all factory owners **exploited** [took advantage of] their workers. Several owners believed that looking after them made sense, because a healthy workforce was likely to be more efficient. Owners like Robert Owen, David Dale and Richard Arkwright looked after their factory hands and still made a profit.

Workers' health was damaged by several factors. Machines were dangerous. Moving parts were not covered. Fingers and limbs were often crushed and left lying on the factory floor. This is what happened to one young boy.

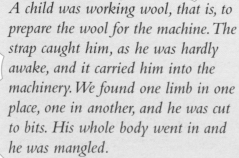

A child was working wool, that is, to prepare the wool for the machine. The strap caught him, as he was hardly awake, and it carried him into the machinery. We found one limb in one place, one in another, and he was cut to bits. His whole body went in and he was mangled.

An illustration showing children working in a factory

Were children treated cruelly, in the new factories?
If you look carefully at this picture you will see some evidence to suggest that children suffered harsh treatment. However, we must remember that the 1800s were very different times to our own. Punishment was much stricter and until the law changed in the 1820s, the death penalty was the punishment for many offences. Public executions still took place until 1868. So, does this information excuse or explain the behaviour of the factory owners? Factory owners wanted to make a profit. To do so they needed workers to produce goods for selling, yet their factories were full of health hazards and potential dangers. Why was it that some owners didn't care about their workers?

The mines
The Industrial Revolution was dependent on coal and metal ores found in the ground. Those who worked in the mines suffered low wages, long hours and appalling conditions. Younger children were used as **trappers**, which meant they spent their time opening and closing the doors for the ventilation system, whilst older children and women **hurried** [moved] coal in baskets. Working hours were long and children could spend up to 12 hours a day far underground in the dark tunnels. Mines were damp, hot and lacked fresh air. All of this was bad enough, but tunnels could collapse and underground explosions and flooding made it very dangerous. The methane gas produced by coal could easily explode if triggered by the flames of the candles miners used to help them see. In 1842 however, the Mines Act stopped women and children from working in the mines.

A trapper crouching in a tunnel

'I get very tired sitting in the dark by the door so I go to sleep ... Nearly a year ago there was an accident and most of us were burned. I was carried home by a man. It hurt very much because most of the skin was burnt off my face' *Phillip Phillips, aged 9, who worked as a trapper in the coal mines in Merthyr.*

---

1 Look at the Trapper in the picture and imagine you are in his place:
   ◆ How would you feel?   ◆ What would you see and hear?
   ◆ What might it be like working in a mine?

2 Read Phillip Phillips's memories of working in a mine. Which of the words he uses would make you feel frightened? Which words would you replace them with to make you feel safe?

3 In pairs, design two posters. One should argue why children should not work long hours in factories and mines. The other poster should argue why it is okay. Think about the points you want to make and write a list to help you. What will your arguments be?

Stopping the revolution

The big changes that made up the Industrial Revolution did not suit everybody. Some did not agree with the changes and were not happy. They were worried that the new, fast machines would take their jobs. Men and women in different parts of Britain, and at different times during the 19th century, tried to stop the changes or at least slow them down. Who were these people and why did they want to stop the Industrial Revolution?

Luddites

Between 1811 and 1816, the textile areas of Britain, such as Derbyshire, saw violence on a serious scale. Factories and workshops were broken into and machinery was burned or smashed. Factory owners were threatened or even killed. But, who were these 'Luddites', and why were they so angry?

The Luddites were textile workers who believed the new machines were a threat to their jobs. Skilled stocking-frame workers found out that some employers were using machines to make cheaper, lower quality stockings. Unskilled workers could run the machines. This meant that the skilled stocking-makers weren't necessary. Workers in Nottinghamshire and Derbyshire responded by destroying the machines that would replace them. The violence soon spread to factories in Lancashire, Cheshire and Yorkshire. These workers were called Luddites because rumours spread about a man called Ned Ludd, who was supposed to lead the violent attacks. In fact, Ned Ludd never existed – he was a myth.

Many of the Luddite attacks were not just because of the machines. Grain shortages pushed up the price of food and, in 1816, a depression in industry led to unemployment and low wages. With empty bellies and falling wages, many of the attacks were the results of explosive anger and frustration. The government decided to act against the machine-breakers. Seventeen were executed after trials at York in 1812, and troops were brought in to patrol other trouble spots. In the short term, machine-breaking did slow the introduction of machines in some areas, but in the long term it had no real effect.

Captain Swing

Factory workers were not the only ones who disagreed with the changes caused by the Industrial Revolution. Between 1830 and 1832 threats like the one in this letter were frequently carried out by farm labourers. Why was this?

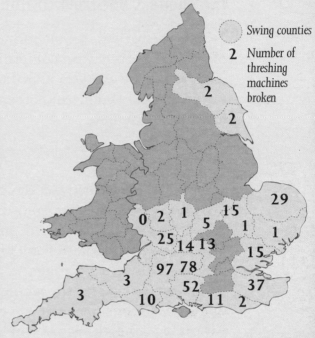

Sir,

This is to let you know that if your threshing machines are not destroyed by you, we shall take action against them ourselves.

Swing

Swing counties

2 Number of threshing machines broken

Like the Luddites, farm labourers were having a very hard time and they also had a mythical leader – Captain Swing. The price of corn was falling, some farmers had lost a lot of money and farm workers had lost their jobs. The winter of 1830 was particularly hard, and many faced starvation. To make matters worse, in the same winter many farmers in the south of England started to use machines for threshing corn. Threshing was one farming job that could be done in the winter, and labourers feared that this would be taken by a machine. Although the new machines did not actually put that many out of work, the labourers saw them as a symbol of their misery. Violence was the result. Hay-ricks were burned, threshing machines were destroyed, and some farmers were injured – all in the name of Captain Swing.

Once more the government acted swiftly. By the middle of 1831 over 1,000 labourers had been tried by 90 courts in 34 different counties of England. 19 men were sentenced to death, 500 were transported to Australia and over 600 were imprisoned.

But, the violence achieved very little. Many labourers continued to live in poverty, and threshing machines were gradually introduced as part of the mechanisation of farming.

---

1 Why do you think the workers used violence instead of peaceful methods to achieve change?

◆ First, make a list of all the words in the text which tell you why the Luddites and the Swing Rioters disagreed with the changes.

◆ On a set of cards, write all the reasons why the Luddites were against machinery. On another set of cards, write the reasons why the Swing Rioters were against machinery.

2 Now, in a group of four, imagine you are either Luddites or Swing Rioters and plan your next attack. Use your cards to help you decide why you think it is necessary to use violence:

◆ Who would be involved?   ◆ How would you attack?

◆ Where and when would the attack be?

3 Why do you think the rioters received such harsh treatment from the authorities?

Coping with the revolution

During the industrial revolution there were some people who may not have agreed with the changes that were happening, but shrugged their shoulders and got on with their lives. These people did not hope to stop the changes but tried to improve their lives instead.

To help themselves, people formed into groups. This seemed the obvious solution. Individual workers who complained about the changes could easily be replaced by an employer, but if workers joined together they could help each other. Some began to organise Trade Unions and others started Friendly Societies or Co-operatives. Let's look at each of these.

Trade Unions

Some well-paid, skilled workers had already organised groups to protect their interests before industrialisation began. These were called trade unions. Other workers now followed suit, but it wasn't easy. Many thought they would be much stronger if they could develop unions which covered the whole country – national unions. More members would give them more bargaining strength against employers. In 1829 John Doherty formed the Grand General Union of Spinners. Two years later a builders' union was started. But all the early large unions failed. Why did this happen?

One reason is that the national unions were too big. Before the railway system developed communication across the country was very difficult. Many workers could not read or write because they had not been to school. It was hard for union leaders to organise action or to get all members to agree on what to do. Some unions refused to support workers in other trades. They didn't believe that other people's disputes had anything to do with them. The government also made things difficult, as it was illegal to form a union until 1825. On top of these problems, running a national union needed money and union subscriptions were hard to collect. Sometimes local union secretaries ran off with the funds!

Later on in the 19th century however, it became easier for national unions to establish themselves, as workers became better educated and the railway system made communication much easier.

A membership card for the Amalgamated Engineers Union

Friendly Societies

There was no welfare state during the period of industrialisation. If you were sick and lost your job or you were unemployed you had to rely on friends, relations or savings. Some workers decided to form 'friendly' societies to try to improve their working lives. They paid regular sums of money into a fund. When times were hard they could then take out payments from the fund. Some friendly societies, such as the Order of Foresters and the Manchester Unity of Oddfellows (both formed in 1833), became national organisations. By 1850, national membership of friendly societies was over 1 million. The friendly societies were good for the well-paid workers who could afford the weekly subscription, but there were many who were paid much less and so couldn't benefit.

Co-operatives

Some people did not want to be part of industrialisation. To stop them from having to join the industrial society by buying its expensive products, they set up **co-operatives**. Shops were set up where goods could be bought cheaply and in bulk, and then sold at low prices to workers. In 1844 twenty-eight weavers invested one pound each to start a shop in Rochdale. They bought and sold goods cheaply and, after paying the running costs, all the profits were shared among the customers according to how much they had bought. The Rochdale Pioneers, as they were called, were the start of something big. By 1870 there were 1,000 co-operatives with 300,000 members. In 1872 local societies combined to form the Co-operative Wholesale Society (CWS). This could buy in massive bulk and at very cheap prices. The CWS started to make some products itself, cutting out the manufacturers' profits completely. The co-operative societies were successful, although its members only made up a fraction of the poor. The CWS still exists today as the Co-op.

A reconstruction of the inside of the Rochdale Co-op

---

1 *Why do you think the early unions failed? Make a list with the most important reason at the top, and the least important reason at the bottom. Explain your decision.*

2 *Why were workers powerless against the owners during industrialisation?*

3 *Why didn't the government step in to help those who suffered during industrialisation?*

4 *What action does the government take today to support vulnerable people?*

Over the last 250 years the Industrial Revolution has improved our living standards enormously. Today we have washing machines, vacuum cleaners and other gadgets which save us time. We have higher incomes and a huge range of goods to choose from. So, all around us we can see the benefits from industrialisation. But, what about the short term – the first 80 to 100 years after 1780? Did the first generation of industrial workers enjoy the benefits of industrialisation or, were they the victims of long hours, low wages and dreadful conditions? Was the Industrial Revolution fantastic or frightful?

1 What do you think 'standard of living' means? Each of the headings below contribute to your standard of living. Decide how important each one is to your life. Give some examples and put them in order of importance. Explain your decisions.

2 If you were investigating the standard of living of British people between 1780 and 1850 what questions would you ask about each heading?

| Wages – how much you earn. | Prices of goods – how much you pay | Health – your physical and mental fitness | Housing conditions – your home |

The debate

Historians do not always agree on what happened in the past. Evidence does not speak for itself, it has to be interpreted and sometimes the same evidence can be viewed in different ways. You are going to decide whether the Industrial Revolution led to higher standards of living between 1780 and 1850. This is the debate about living standards:

*We supporters think that workers at the time **benefited** from the Industrial Revolution.*

SUPPORTERS

*No, no, we believe that workers at the time **suffered**, because of the Industrial Revolution.*

CRITICS

3 Draw up a table, like the one below. Look at the sources and decide with a partner which column each one would best belong in.

Supporters	Critics	Both Views

A

The historian Roderick Floud pointed out that in 1870, new recruits to the Navy were much taller than new recruits had been in 1770. He argues that this was probably because there was a lot more food available by 1870, and so the diets of the working classes were much better than they had been in 1770.

B

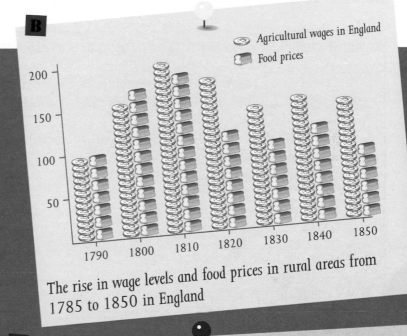

- Agricultural wages in England
- Food prices

The rise in wage levels and food prices in rural areas from 1785 to 1850 in England

C

Of all the workers who compete against machinery, the ones who suffer the most are the handloom weavers in the cotton industry. These workers receive the lowest wages. They consider themselves lucky if they can earn between 6 and 7 shillings a week for 14 to 18 hours a day spent behind the loom.

Friedrich Engels writing about handloom weavers in 1844

D

Between 1780 and 1850 the wages of skilled workers doubled and the wages of those doing non-manual jobs increased four times. Also, the population seems to have got taller, which shows that people's diets improved.

But, there were differences across the country. In Glasgow the wages of better paid, skilled workers improved but unskilled workers wages stayed the same. Agricultural workers in the south and east of Britain also did very badly between 1780 and 1850.

Some of the ideas of the historian Eric Evans (1996)

4 Which column on your chart did you put Eric Evans in?

5 Which sources contain evidence that support Eric Evans' conclusions about standards of living? Are there any conclusions that are not supported by the sources?

6 Use all the evidence to plan and write your answer to the question — did the Industrial Revolution lead to higher standards of living between 1780 and 1850? Back up your answer using all the sources.

Today, people make money out of history, and the heritage industry is a business. In Britain in the late 1960s there were 800 museums, today we have 2,000. Museums are becoming big business and a large number focus on the Industrial Revolution – 464 museums have industrial material of some kind on display.

A museum curator has asked you to help them set up an exhibition on life in an industrial town.

1 Make a list of 5 things you **would** expect to see in a museum, and 5 things you **would not** expect to see in a museum. First, we should think about the role of museums.

2 *As a class, think of any museum you have visited recently, then discuss each of the statements below. Do you agree with any of them?*

Museums should:

- ◆ entertain the public who pay to see them;
- ◆ provide information about the past;
- ◆ show what life was like in the past.

3 You will see glimpses of two museums below. Compare your knowledge of industrialisation with the way it has been presented by these museums. Using the chart below, give each museum a score out of 5 for each of the points you have discussed – you could also include your own ideas about museums. Justify your decision using your knowledge of the Industrial Revolution.

Museum name:		
Museums should ...	**Score out of 5**	**Score given because ...**
Entertain		
Inform		
Show what life was like		

The Peak District Mining Museum

This museum opened in 1978 and celebrates the long history of mining in Derbyshire. Inside the museum there are glass displays with pictures and explanations showing how lead was mined and brought to the surface. You can also watch slide shows which tell you all about mining. The museum booklet tells you that the miner usually wore clogs and that they used candles to help them see what they were doing. It goes on to say:

"underground was wet and muddy in most cases, so he [the miner] suffered from rheumatism and **respiratory** [breathing] problems – sometimes the air was so bad that the candle had to be placed some distance behind him to avoid going out."

Industrial Revolution?

Children looking at mining machinery

A 19th century coal wagon being pushed through a tunnel

Visitors listening to a talk on mining tools

The Beamish Museum

This museum tells the story of life in the North of England between 1800 and 1900. The guide book explains that the purpose of the museum is to 'make the history of a region live.' The museum is a living and working museum. This means that it recreates the past exactly as it would have been, with working buildings and people dressed as they would have done at the time. You can visit a mining village, attend a lesson in the school and go down a mine to see what life was really like. There are no glass cases and very few labels. The owners feel that objects should be seen as they would have been at the time, and that labels and glass cases would get in the way of this. Instead, they advise visitors to 'talk to people in the buildings who are trained to talk to visitors and answer questions.'

A 19th century photograph of a coal miner. He has bandy legs due to a disease called rickets.

A member of staff operating a steam winder

Two of the staff checking the weight of the tubs of coal

4 Bearing in mind the scores you gave to each museum, you can now plan your exhibition.

◆ What story would you want to tell?

◆ What aspects of life do you want to show?

◆ What items would you choose to show and why?

◆ How will you present working conditions?

◆ How would you show them?

◆ Which pictures from this book would you use?

5 Draw up a storyboard to plan your exhibition.

The growth of the British Empire

By 1900 the British Empire covered nearly one quarter of the world. Some *colonies* had been part of the empire before 1750, but the majority were added during the years of the Industrial Revolution, 1750–1900. So, where was the British Empire in 1900? How and why did it grow? And did British rule benefit or harm the countries and peoples in the empire?

FACT FILE

◆ A **colony** is a country or a region, which is under the control, or influence, of a more powerful country.

◆ An **empire** is a group of colonies, which are controlled by one powerful country.

Look at the three maps on the next few pages. They show how the British and other European empires changed between 1763 and 1900. As you look at the maps think about how you would answer these questions.

1 Between which dates did the British Empire grow fastest?

2 What changed between 1763, 1800 and 1900? What stayed the same? Make a list of all the changes and things that stayed the same, under the headings '1763', '1800' and '1900.'

3 Who were Britain's European rivals in 1763, 1800 and 1900?

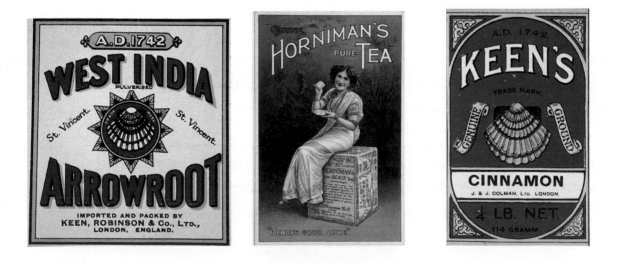

A selection of products produced in the empire, and available to buy in Britain in the late 1800s.

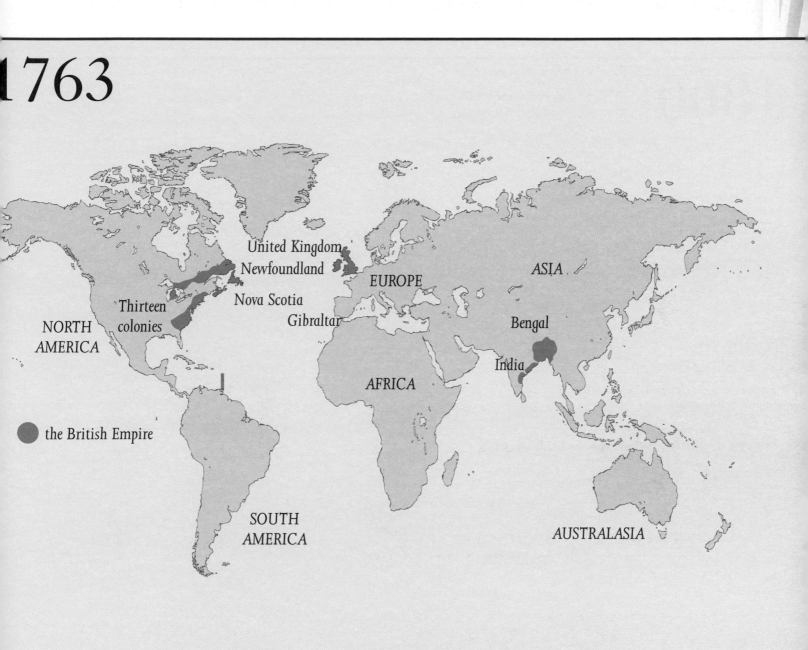

United Kingdom
Newfoundland
Nova Scotia
Gibraltar

EUROPE

ASIA

Bengal

India

NORTH AMERICA

Thirteen colonies

AFRICA

the British Empire

SOUTH AMERICA

AUSTRALASIA

Britain's empire was created over a long period of time. As you can see, in 1763 the empire was relatively small. Some countries became part of the empire because of wars, some were 'discovered' by Britons, and others had a lot of British people already living there. Other countries became part of the empire because of trade – merchants gained a lot of power from trading in places like India. In this section of the book, we will be looking at how the empire grew, as well as how the empire affected people in the different countries.

1800

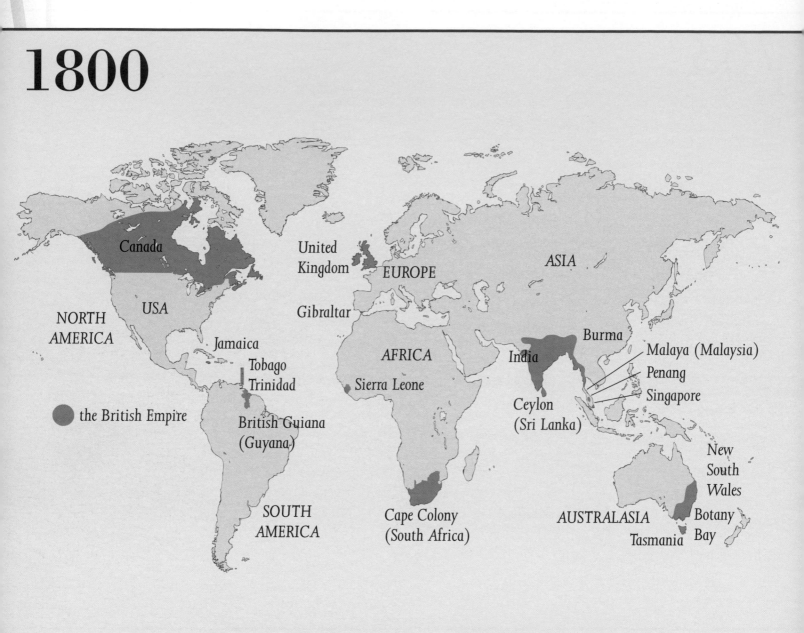

The Industrial Revolution that took place in Britain between 1750 and 1900 depended upon trade with other countries. Very many raw materials could not be grown in Britain because of the climate. But tobacco and sugar could grow in the Americas, and cotton, tea and spices flourished in India. Trading companies sent ships to these places to buy raw materials and bring them back to Britain. The companies set up trading posts abroad because having local bases made it easier to sell goods made in Britain, and to buy raw materials from the colony.

By 1900 the British Empire was the largest in the world. It included countries in every continent and made up nearly one quarter of the world. As the British Empire stretched over such a large area it was called 'the empire on which the sun never sets,' because whatever position the sun was in, it was shining on some part of the British Empire.

1900

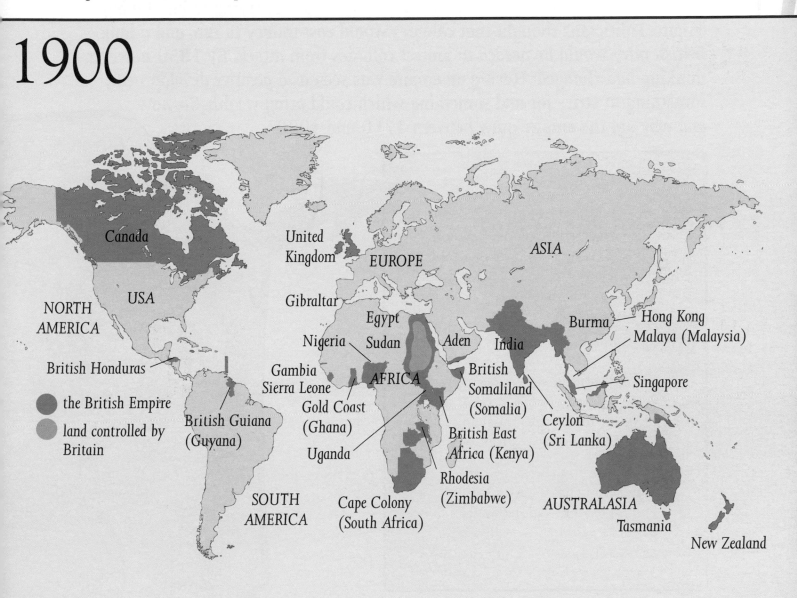

Canada

United Kingdom

EUROPE

ASIA

NORTH AMERICA

USA

Gibraltar

Egypt

Burma

Hong Kong
Malaya (Malaysia)

Nigeria

Sudan

Aden

India

British Honduras

Gambia
Sierra Leone

AFRICA

British
Somaliland
(Somalia)

Singapore

the British Empire

land controlled by Britain

British Guiana
(Guyana)

Gold Coast
(Ghana)

Uganda

British East
Africa (Kenya)

Ceylon
(Sri Lanka)

Rhodesia
(Zimbabwe)

SOUTH
AMERICA

Cape Colony
(South Africa)

AUSTRALASIA

Tasmania

New Zealand

Why did the empire grow?

During the 18th century the British government was not trying to build a big empire. Politicians thought that colonies would cost money to run, and a large British navy would be needed to protect colonies from attack. By 1850 however, thinking had changed. Having an empire was seen as a positive development, something to strive for and something which could bring wealth. So, how and why did the empire grow between 1750 and 1900?

Winning wars

Britain often fought wars against her European rivals, and usually won. As part of the peace treaty, Britain gained colonies from rivals. This was one way in which the empire grew larger.

FACT FILE

◆ Britain won the Seven Years' War against France (1756–1763). As a result, Britain took Canadian and French trading posts in India.

◆ After winning the battle of Waterloo in 1815, against the French leader, Napoleon, Britain gained Ceylon (now called Sri Lanka) and part of South Africa.

Spreading Christianity

Many Christians in Britain thought the beliefs of people in the colonies were 'uncivilised' and 'barbaric'. Some of them travelled to the colonies to try and make people believe in Christianity. We call these people **missionaries**. They sometimes worked in colonies alongside merchants, but in other places they were on their own. Missionaries helped to establish a British presence in Africa, India and China.

A decorative plate, made in 1887 to celebrate Queen Victoria's Golden Jubilee year and the British Empire

42

Exploring and emigration

Some parts of the empire were won accidentally. Captain James Cook landed in New Zealand and Australia and claimed both for Britain. Of course, people had lived there for many years before his arrival, but Cook was considered to be an explorer because he was the first European to land there. However, the steady stream of **emigrants** [people who go to live in another place] from Britain, and the superior weapons of the British, ensured that any opposition by the native Aborigines and Maoris was quickly put down.

Helping trade

Some colonies were conquered to help British trade. In 1842, the British took control of Hong Kong, following a war during which the Chinese were forced to accept opium as payment for tea, porcelain and silk. In 1882, the British invaded Egypt to ensure the important trade route through the Suez Canal was protected from the rival French.

Protecting the colonies

After 1750, Britain's navy grew in size so that it could protect British ships trading with other countries. It was also able to defend colonies from attack by European rivals. The government wanted to keep ahead of other countries, so it tried to maintain a navy that was as big as the combined navies of her main competitors.

---

1 Which of the causes of the growth of the empire do you think were linked together? How are they linked?

2 Make a list for a ruler who wants to build an empire, titled '10 steps to building an empire'.

In 1600 the British East India Company was established in London. The merchants who put up the money to start the company wanted a share of the trade in spices with the **East Indies** [Southeast Asia]. However, the Dutch beat them to it, so they turned their attention to India. Over the next two hundred years, the power of the company grew, until it controlled most of India. But, how could this happen?

In India, most people who worked for the East India Company were traders. They bought and sold Indian textiles and spices and handled the company's accounts. Some other people who worked for the company were soldiers, sailors, doctors and priests. It was difficult for the East India Company's owners in Britain to control what was happening in India, and sometimes people got greedy and became very rich indeed. One employee, Warren Hastings who was also the first Governor-General of India, made his fortune by corrupt and dishonest means.

At the end of the 18th century, Parliament stepped in and the East India Company was brought under its control. In the next hundred years, two developments happened which made it possible for the company to expand its influence in India. First, the Mughal rulers of India lost control of the country, and individual princes took over different parts of it to rule by themselves. The second development was that French traders seemed to pose a threat to the East India Company. So, British troops and ships were sent to drive them out. After a series of battles the French were defeated. Why did the British attempt to extend their power? Listen to what Robert Clive has to say about this. He was one of the company's key men in India in 1759.

*If Britain conquers Bengal, Bombay and Madras, all three areas would be a source of huge wealth for Britain. Our influence over our European rivals would also be greatly increased. We will only need a small number of soldiers from Britain because we can also make use of **sepoys** [Indian soldiers], who would rather fight for us because they get better pay and treatment than they do from any Indian ruler.*

The East India Company acted on behalf of the British Government in India. But, in 1858 the company was abolished and India was ruled directly by Britain through a **Viceroy** [a governor]. This was because of events in 1857. In that year, many sepoys and Indian civilians rebelled against the company with acts of great cruelty on both sides. After the defeat of the rebels, the fate of India was sealed: it was now part of the British Empire.

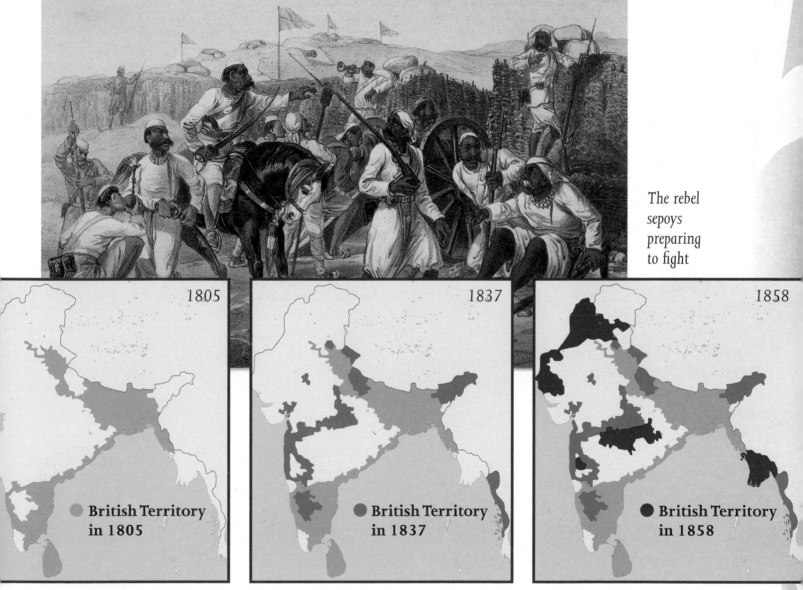

The rebel sepoys preparing to fight

1805

● **British Territory in 1805**

1837

● **British Territory in 1837**

1858

● **British Territory in 1858**

The growth of British control in India

1   List four key words which show why Robert Clive thought it was important for Britain to gain control in India.

2   Who else might have been keen to see British control in India?

3   What factors enabled the British to take over India? What factors made them attempt to do so?

India was once called the 'Jewel in the Crown' of the British Empire. Since 1947, when India achieved independence, arguments have raged about the legacy left by the British. Some say that India benefited from British rule, others are sure it did more harm than good. In this section you are going to make up your own mind on this issue.

The East India Company plundered India, they looted it. The taxes that were collected from Indian people paid for further wars of conquest!

*I don't disagree, but it wasn't all bad. The authorities did abolish **sutee** [the burning of widows on their husbands' funeral pyres] in 1829, and eventually established a nationwide postal service to help improve communications. And what about the legal system that the British introduced?*

Yes, the legal system was new but it was very expensive, and most Indians couldn't afford to use it. Of course, there were some Indians who benefited from British rule, but these were the Indian princes, the landlords and the professionals who benefited from the western education. They were only a tiny minority of the population.

I disagree. The railway network the British built did help everyone in India, especially in times of food shortages. It also helped the British as they could transport materials and goods more easily.

Really? Let's look at the evidence shall we?

1 Look at the sources below and, with a partner, decide if railways were built **a)** for Britain's benefit, **b)** for India's benefit, or **c)** for the benefit of both Britain and India.

District	Before railway	After railway
Dinajpur	30.8 rupees	20.2 rupees
Mymensingh	20.3 rupees	13.7 rupees

The price of rice in two districts of Bengal before and after the arrival of the railway.

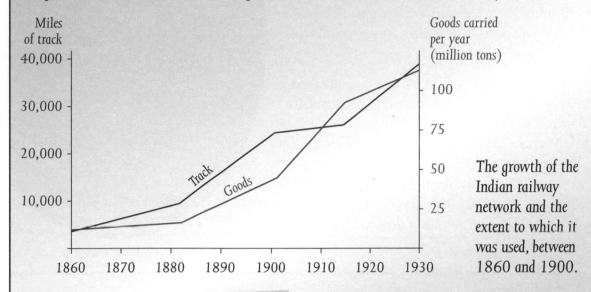

The growth of the Indian railway network and the extent to which it was used, between 1860 and 1900.

Indians criticised the British government in India for wasting money on railways. If a similar amount had been spent on irrigation it would have benefited Indian agriculture and increased its productivity. The British did not listen to this criticism — they did not spend much on irrigation and went ahead with the railway. The expansion of the Indian railways created an enormous demand for steel (rails and bridges), engines, wagons and even English coal. As all of this was imported from Britain, it did not benefit Indians.

Historian, Dietmar Rothermund, 1988

India's railway system had a huge impact on the Indian economy. It created an engineering industry that would provide the basis for a lot of India's economic development. It also made it possible for a lot of people to move around the country. Railways made it possible for nationalist leaders to move freely about the country. Finally, the railways made it possible to control half a continent with a relatively small, but mobile, army.

Historian, David Fieldhouse, 1996

2 What are the key differences in the views of the modern historians?

3 Which historian do you support? Give your reasons.

Explorers 'find' and claim new lands

One of the reasons why the empire expanded between 1750 and 1900 was because Britons began to explore parts of the world which had not been seen by white people before. As a result of these explorations, parts of the world became colonies of the British Empire.

James Cook was one of these explorers. He made three voyages, and made maps of the Pacific Ocean, which no European had done before. He claimed Australia and New Zealand for Britain, in spite of the fact that people were living there already.

Once news of Cook's voyages reached Britain it inspired merchants, missionaries and settlers to travel to Australia and New Zealand. The British government took an interest too. Convicts who were sentenced to transportation usually sailed for the American colonies, but in 1786 the government decided to try out the new site in Australia, which was called New South Wales. In January 1788, eleven ships carrying more than 1300 people, including convicts, soldiers and crews landed at Botany Bay.

The British explorer, Captain James Cook

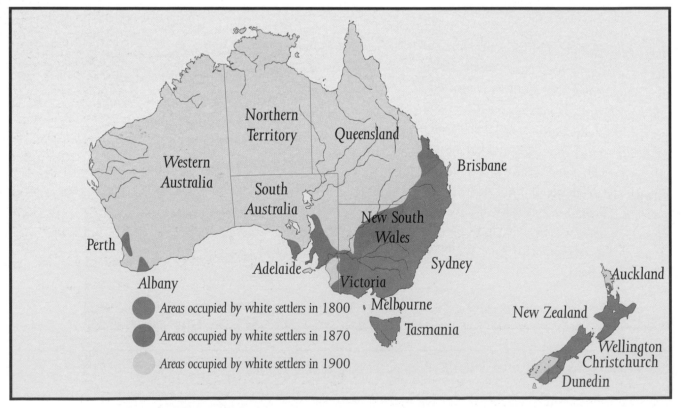

The growth of British settlement in Australia

The early years of settlement in Australia were harsh. The newcomers had to suffer crop failures, drought and floods. But a second fleet in 1790 and a third in 1791, helped the little colony to survive. However, all this harmed the local Aborigines. Violence erupted with killings on both sides, and by 1792 the British had put down roots in Sydney, Australia.

During the 19th century the government tried to encourage emigration from Britain, to increase the number of British people abroad. One of the most popular destinations was Australia. Women in particular were encouraged to emigrate, because Australia contained a lot more men. A gold rush in the 1850s encouraged others to leave Britain and seek their fortune. Between 1815 and 1914, about 2 million British people settled in Australia.

A painting of British emigrants leaving Britain for Australia. The painting is called 'A primrose from England'.

1 The number of Aborigines that met the first British settlers was small. Why didn't the British respect their rights?

2 Given what you know about conditions in Britain during the Industrial Revolution, why do you think so many people wanted to emigrate?

The Scramble for Africa

By 1870, most of the world had become a colony of one European country or another – apart from Africa. But, between 1880 and 1914, European powers divided up the continent of Africa with breathtaking speed. The Scramble for Africa, as it is called, was not a series of successful battles and conquests, as had happened elsewhere in the world during this period of empire building. It was more like a frantic race between competing powers. You are going to investigate why the Europeans wanted a share of Africa, and what happened during the Scramble for Africa.

Britain had trade links with Africa going back many years to the time of the slave trade. British missionaries had also been working in Africa for many years. Disregarding the customs and beliefs of the Africans they met, the missionaries tried to 'civilise' the African people by teaching them Christianity. More recently, in South Africa, the British had taken control of the Cape Colony from the Dutch. But, from the middle of the 19th century, many European explorers began to look more closely at Africa. Before this time, it was only the coast of Africa that was known to Europeans. Explorers, such as David Livingstone, began to investigate the middle of Africa, making maps of the country.

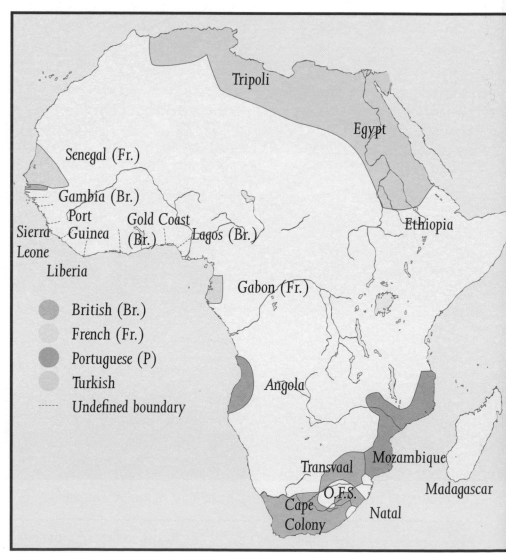

Africa in 1880

50

Diamonds and gold

These explorations made the European powers realise the importance of Africa. In Southern Africa, the discovery of diamonds in 1867 and gold in 1886 made the continent even more attractive for Europeans. All the European countries were beginning to catch up with Britain's Industrial Revolution, and all were looking for new markets and new materials. Africa could easily provide these. Suddenly, Africa became more important than ever before.

The opening of the Suez Canal in Egypt in 1869 made the security of Egypt very important in the eyes of the British. The country that had control over the Suez Canal had control over the trade route to India – and this was vital for Britain as India was the 'jewel in the crown'. In 1882 the British invaded Egypt to stop the financial collapse of the country. The British also fought against the **Boers** [Dutch settlers] in the Boer War of 1899, to control South Africa and the wealth it contained. In fact, a lot of the Scramble for Africa was about countries stopping rivals, or potential rivals, from taking land that they thought they might be interested in themselves.

If you look at the map below you can see how the continent of Africa was divided up by 1914.

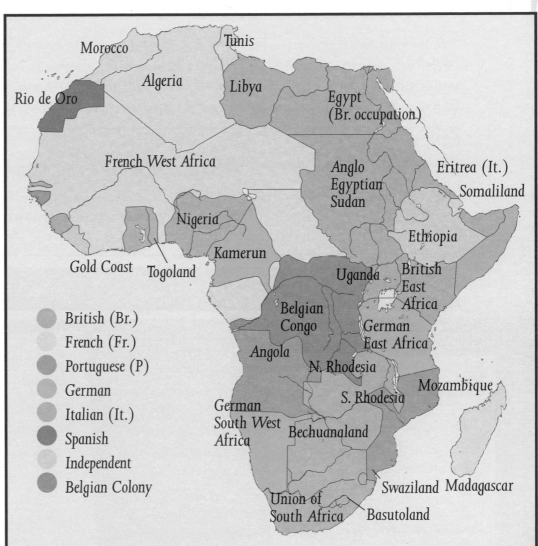

The European division of Africa by 1914

The Scramble for Africa divided the majority of the continent between the European powers. Britain's colonies stretched across Africa from west to east, and from north to south. But, did Britain's African colonies benefit from being part of the empire?

You have been asked by your local museum to design an exhibition about this period of British history. A number of artefacts, posters and other sources have been lent to you for display. You can add to them if you like from other books or the Internet. The title of your display is: 'Did the British Empire harm or help its African colonies?'

---

1 Look at each exhibit and read the captions carefully.

◆ Arrange your exhibits under three headings: **Commerce**, **Christianity**, and **Conquest**. You may want to use the exhibits more than once.

◆ The exhibits you choose and the way you arrange them, should answer the question — did the British Empire harm or help its African colonies?

Did the British Empire harm or help its African colonies?

THE RHODES COLOSSUS
STRIDING FROM CAPE TOWN TO CAIRO.

A cartoon of Cecil Rhodes, standing over the whole continent of Africa, 1892. Rhodes was Prime Minister of the Cape Colony and developer of Rhodesia (Zimbabwe).

I look for some reason why I should obey you, and find not the smallest. If you want friendship, then I am ready for it, today and always. But to be your subject — that I cannot be. If it is war you want, then I am ready for that, but never to be your subject. I am chief here in my land. You are chief in your land. But listen: I do not say that you must obey me, for I know that you are a free man.

The Yao chief, Mazemba, said this upon meeting Europeans.

A sun of disaster has risen in the West. Glaring down on people and populated places. Poetically speaking, I mean the catastrophe of the Christians. The Christian calamity has come upon us Like a dust cloud.

A poem by an African poet

THE LION'S JUST SHARE.

This cartoon was published in 1882, and shows the European powers competing for a part of Africa. The lion represents Britain.

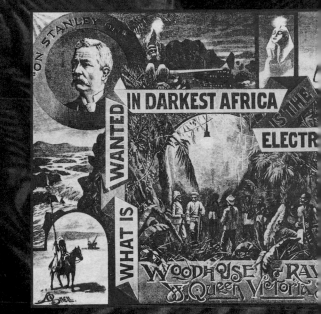

A British company advertising how it can bring electric light to 'darkest' Africa

A baptism in the Lower Congo. Missionaries brought Christianity and education to Africa in an attempt to 'civilise' the African people.

The British legal system comes to Africa. A trial of a West African at a British court in the 1890s.

2 After finishing your exhibition, what conclusion did you reach?

3 A reporter from the local newspaper has come to interview you about your exhibition. Write an interview between you and the reporter, explaining why and how you reached your decision. Try to include the words below in your report.

◆ Missionary ◆ Civilise ◆ Education ◆ Battle ◆ Slave ◆ Government

The expanding empire: child migration

Britain exports girls and boys!

Imagine you read this headline today in a newspaper. You probably wouldn't believe it. You would look at the date to check it wasn't April Fool's Day instead. How could it happen? Well, it doesn't happen now, but in our very recent history it did.

You have already seen that by 1900 Britain had a large empire, of which the British people were very proud. In many colonies the British used the local people to work on farms and construct railways and roads. But, in some colonies, such as Australia, Canada and New Zealand there was a shortage of labour. At the same time, Britain was suffering from high unemployment. To fill the jobs in the colonies, and to ease unemployment problems at home, over 150,000 children were exported from Britain.

Child migration, as it was called, was meant to be carried out in the best interests of the children, but did the children's interests really come first? What were the reasons for the child migration schemes? Was child migration something the British Empire should be proud of?

Study the sources on these pages, to help you decide who benefited more – the children or the empire.

SOURCE 1

I believe that London has become too full of children. There has been a great increase in child crime. I blame the lack of employment for people between the ages of 12 and 20 for this. I therefore suggest migration as a remedy.

Adapted from a police report published in 1826 about emigration from Britain

SOURCE 2

Take them away! Take them away!
The **bountiful** [generous] earth is wide and free,
The New shall repair the wrongs of the Old –
God be with them over the sea!

Part of a poem called 'The Departures of the Innocents' written in the 19th century

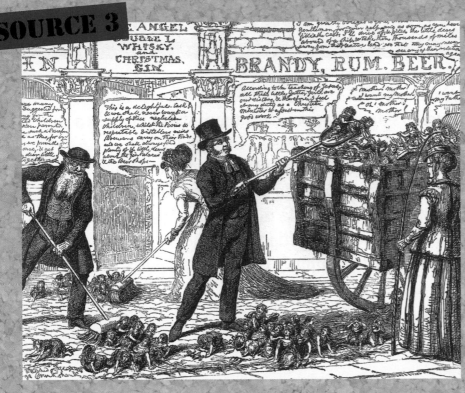

A cartoon called 'Our Gutter Children' from the magazine Punch, drawn in 1869 by George Cruikshank

SOURCE 4

Well-planned and wisely conducted child-emigration, especially to Canada, is the best solution to some of Britain's biggest problems. It will also help our colonies. First, it relieves the overcrowded city centres and unemployment at home. Second, it supplies what the colonies need most — an increase of the English-speaking population. Third, it provides the children with unspeakable blessings.

Adapted from the memoirs of Thomas John Barnardo, explaining why he sent children in his care abroad

1 List the words in the sources which suggest that children were seen as 'problems'. Why do you think this was?

2 The people who organised child migration did so for different reasons. Explain what these reasons were under the headings below. Which reason seems to be the most important?

Social reasons	Economic reasons	Religious reasons

3 Who do you think benefited the most from child migration? Give your reasons.

Was child migration a good scheme?

Mention the name Barnardo's and what do you think of? Charity? Help for children? Today, the Barnardo's organisation helps thousands of children and young people to lead a better life. But, between 1882 and 1914, several organisations sent around 20,000 children to Canada and other countries in the empire. Thomas Barnardo, Annie MacPherson and Maria Rye were some of the people who ran these child migration schemes. Using Barnardo as an example, you are going to investigate whether or not these children benefited from being part of the empire's migration schemes.

Thomas John Barnardo

Born: 4 July 1845 in Dublin, Ireland.

At the age of 17 Barnardo converted to evangelical Christianity so that he could become a missionary in China. Rejected because he was too headstrong, Barnardo started preaching in the East End of London and founded a **mission** [shelter] for children. In 1872, after hearing the story of a homeless and starving boy called Jim Jarvis, and seeing the plight of London's homeless children for himself, Barnardo founded a home for children like Jim. Since then, the organisation he founded – Barnardo's – has helped thousands of children.

Sending children abroad saved money. During the 1880s an economic depression hit Britain, and Barnardo's message seemed very sensible. Barnardo received large donations to finance the scheme, and child migration went ahead. Many child migrants have been interviewed and nearly all of them say that the migration schemes did them no harm, and perhaps some good.

We have seen some of Barnardo's reasons for child migration on the previous pages. Barnardo also said:

> I am amazed at the unwillingness of the government to agree a small amount of money for the maintenance of children in one of our colonies. The cost is half the yearly amount that is already being spent on keeping the same children in England.

1 Look back at Sources 1–4 on pages 54–55. Considering these sources and the information so far, do you think that, at the time, the migration schemes seemed good for the children?

2 If they did, why do you think this was? If not, why not?

Was everybody happy?

It seems from the evidence that the schemes were successful. But, not all child migrants enjoyed their new homes in the colonies. There is evidence to suggest that even if the children weren't asking to go, they still had to.

It was explained that the opportunities for a happy and prosperous life would be much better... Actually, we did not want to be sent anywhere. I was quite content to stay in jolly England, even though England had not been so jolly lately.

One thirteen year-old boy remembered being called into the main office of his Children's Home.

A group of Barnardo's children leaving for Canada in the early 1900s

---

3 Considering this new information, do you think that, at the time, the migration schemes seemed good for the children? If they did, why do you think this was? If not, why not?

4 Did everybody have the same opinion?

In the 19th century the law did not allow children to be taken from their parents even if they were being badly treated. Barnardo took the law into his own hands. He argued that he had the right to save children from being harmed. There were many times when Barnardo ended up in the High Court facing demands for the return of neglected children he had taken without consent. So, it could be argued that Barnardo was rescuing children.

---

5 After looking at all the information, have your opinions changed?

6 Imagine you were alive at the time, would you think the schemes were good or bad for the children? In pairs, debate this question. One of you should argue the 'good' side, the other should argue the 'bad' side.

7 Annie MacPherson and Maria Rye ran two of the other child migration schemes. Using the library and the internet, investigate these organisations. Were these schemes similar to Barnardo's? What were their motives?

In 1988, the Barnardo organisation said that its policy of sending children abroad was part of a period of history, a stage in its development as a charity. It would be entirely wrong to do the same thing today. The organisation felt that Barnardo's actions should not be judged in terms of today's values. You can see from this that it is often important for historians to judge evidence and events using the standards of the period, rather than using modern opinions.

Images of war: Zulus and soldiers

The Zulu Kingdom was located on the eastern coast of Southern Africa. British explorers and traders were attracted to the area in their search for land, raw materials and trade. A British colony was set up in Natal, right on the Zulu border. By the 1870s, the British government was using military force to bring all the different ethnic groups in Southern Africa together, under its control.

British attempts to conquer the area met with resistance from the native Zulu forces. On 22 January 1879, the main unit of British soldiers was badly defeated by the Zulus at Isandhlwana. Following the battle, on the same day, the reserve Zulu army decided to attack Rorke's Drift – a supply depot on the British border. For 12 hours, eighty-four British soldiers held the Zulus at bay and finally fought them off. Eleven Victoria Crosses were later awarded to the British soldiers. As a result, the defence of Rorke's Drift has gone down in history as an example of British heroism.

---

1 Look at the picture below. Elizabeth Butler painted this because Queen Victoria asked her to portray the gallant defence of Rorke's Drift.

◆ Describe the scene in ten words.

◆ What does it tell you about how Victoria wanted people in the future to remember Rorke's Drift?

Elizabeth Butler planned her painting carefully. For a start, some of the 'main heroes' were available for her to study. They were asked to re-enact their part in the action, dressed in the uniforms they had worn on the day. Butler's aim was to include portraits of all eleven men who were awarded the Victoria Cross.

In 1965, Cy Endfield directed the film *Zulu*. Here are two stills from the film. The publicity surrounding the film did a lot to draw the public's attention to the defence of Rorke's Drift.

The Zulus' attack on Rorke's Drift

The film suggests that the Zulus took the rifles from the bodies of dead soldiers at Isandhlwana, to use at Rorke's Drift.

 This can't have happened. The damage to Rorke's Drift was not the type of damage caused by rifles.

The brave soldiers

At the end of the film, the Zulus are seen saluting the soldiers who bravely defended Rorke's Drift.

FACT This is not true. Both sides were exhausted at the end of a long night of fighting. When the Zulus saw extra British troops arriving, they retreated. In fact, when the battle was over, the remaining British soldiers shot and bayonetted any surviving, wounded Zulus they found on the battlefield.

2 What are the similarities between the painting and the stills?

3 How are the Zulus presented in the stills and the painting? Give examples to support your answer.

4 Having read about the battle on these two pages, can you trust the pictures and stills as historical evidence? Explain your answer.

How great was the British Empire?

You have seen some of the main changes that took place in the British Empire between 1750 and 1900. But, overall, were all the changes positive? Just how 'great' was the British Empire?

To make your decision you need to consider what the word 'great' means to you. Here are some ideas to get you started.

◆ 'Great' could mean 'powerful'. Was the British Empire the most powerful in the world? How can power be measured? Navies? Armies? Empires?

◆ Or was the empire 'great' because Britain had certain 'civilised' standards and British people lived in a fair society? For example, were justice, fairness, and the rule of law accepted and put into practice?

◆ You could use the description 'great' in these ways or think of your own definitions by using dictionaries and the internet.

1 Look at each of the sources below and give each one a mark out of ten, where **1** means you think it doesn't provide evidence to support the empire being 'great'; **10** means you think it does.

◆ You will need to think about the meaning of 'great' and apply it to the empire in comparison with other countries. You should also think about 'great' in terms of Britain's relations with the colonies that formed its empire by 1900.

SOURCE 1

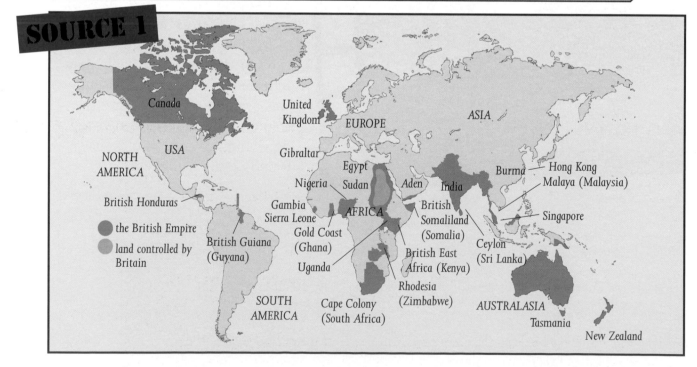

The empire of Britain in 1900

A cartoonist's view of Europeans grabbing land. Britain demands the **'lion's share'** [the biggest share]

	Austria-Hungary	France	Germany	Great Britain	Italy	Japan	Russia	USA
Population	45m	39m	56m	42m	32m	44m	133m	76m
Soldiers	397,000	590,000	585,000	281,000	262,000	273,000	860,000	71,000
Number of battleships	0	13	14	38	9	6	13	17

The population, number of soldiers in the regular army and the number of battleships, in eight countries in 1900

SOURCE 4

To us – to us, and not to others, a certain duty has been assigned. To carry light and civilization in the dark places of the world; to touch the mind of Asia and of Africa with the ethical ideas of Europe.

Part of an article written in 1897, by H.W. Wyatt

SOURCE 5

In everything that makes a people great, in colonizing power, in trade and commerce, in all the higher arts of civilization, England not only excels all other nations of the modern world, but all nations in ancient history as well.

The Canadian, Sir Wilfred Laurier, wrote this about England, 1897

2 Arrange your sources in rank order. What did you decide overall?

◆ The source which provides the strongest evidence is _____ because _____.

◆ The source which provides the weakest evidence is _____ because _____.

◆ The choice was easy / hard because _____.

4 Summarise your decisions by writing an answer to the question: 'The British Empire: both great and civilised.' How accurate is this description of Britain and its treatment of its colonies in 1900?

◆ You should use the information on pages 38–61 to support your answer and include arguments for both sides.

Meet the middle classes

Between 1750 and 1900 the middle classes rapidly increased their number and grew in importance. In 1831, Lord Henry Brougham described them as 'the wealth and intelligence of the country, the glory of the British name'. They were the people who built the businesses that were at the heart of the Industrial Revolution and the growth of the British Empire. But, who were these people?

The middle classes were made up of many different types of people, so finding out what class a person was is not easy. To help you here are some guidelines:

◆ The **upper class** did not have to work – their income came from their land and property;

◆ the **middle class** did work, but generally not with their hands;

◆ the **working class** worked with their hands.

> **1** Look at the people below. Decide which of them are middle class and which are working class. Explain your decisions.

Richard Arkwright

A farm labourer

*This is me and some of my family taking a break from the harvest. Between my wife and I, our weekly earnings come to about **8s and 6d** [about £50 today] with better money at harvest time. Our weekly expenses add up to 8s and 11d so we don't have a lot left over after pay-day.*

My father was a tailor so I learned a lot about cloth from him. I knew from talking to others that the cloth industry needed a faster way of spinning the yarn for the weavers to use. In 1768 I made my own spinning machine and built a factory to house lots of them. I became very rich and using the profit from my business I built other factories and bought a country estate. In 1786 King George III gave me a Knighthood.

This is my family. We all work together making wire brushes at home. If we can sell them all then we can buy food, but sometimes not all the brushes are sold.

A family at work

Sake Deen Mahomed

*Although I was born in India I came to Britain with my employer, Captain Baker, an army officer. I live in Brighton and there, in 1801, I set up a business providing indoor baths with hot and cold sea-water for people who suffer from **rheumatic** [joint] pains. I also introduced 'shampooing' to the British people. My fame soon spread, and King George IV made me Supervisor of the Royal Baths in Brighton. I have even published a book, describing my cures for asthma, rheumatism and lumbago.*

I am a chemist and this is my shop. I sell pills, lotions, tonics and creams to my customers. I work long hours to build up my shop and make a name for myself.

A chemist

My Mum sent me out to work in these brickworks. Her job didn't bring in enough money so I'm having to make bricks to earn a bit for the family.

A young brick-maker in Staffordshire

What jobs did the middle classes do?

On the previous pages you have seen some of the people that we call 'middle class'. During the 19th century the numbers of middle-class people increased rapidly. What jobs did these people do and why were they important?

Middle-class jobs

◆ Merchants were middle-class people. They traded goods at home and abroad. Merchants were selling and buying long before 1750, but they expanded in numbers and importance because of industrialisation. The factory owners needed to find new customers for the goods they were producing. During the 19th century, merchants found these new customers all over the growing British Empire.

◆ Manufacturers and industrialists were also middle class and they too increased in number because of Industrialisation. As the Industrial Revolution progressed, raw materials from the colonies of the British Empire were shipped to factories in Britain to be processed. The finished goods were sold all around the world. All of this made Britain rich, and encouraged others to join the manufacturing boom.

◆ Before 1750 anyone following a career in the law the army or the Church was a middle-class professional. As the population grew, the cities developed and the Industrial Revolution took off, the number of jobs and professions multiplied. People became mechanical and civil engineers, accountants and surveyors. They provided service for people with their own property. These middle class professionals also grew in status. The Law Society was established in 1825 to represent and support solicitors and barristers. In 1837 architec began their own organisations, as did pharmacist in 1841 and mechanical engineers in 1847.

Clerks [book-keepers], office workers, transport workers, shopkeepers, and tradesmen of all kinds were needed in the new industries to fill the new roles. The number of clerks, for example, climbed from 30,000 in 1803 to 90,000 in 1861. By 1891 there were 370,000 male clerks and 19,000 female clerks. During this period it became more and more acceptable for women to work. Women could work in many new jobs – as telephonists, for example.

As you can see, the middle classes filled a wide variety of different occupations. Despite their differences, they did share some common characteristics.

Common characteristics

1 They did work, but not with their hands.

2 They had homes of their own which they usually rented. Houses were of a decent size and in a 'suitable' location – not in the working-class industrial areas.

3 They often had at least one servant.

4 They had money leftover after paying for the basics such as food, clothing and shelter. This was spent on a variety of new goods, such as coffee, which were either made in Britain or came from the Empire.

---

1 *Which middle-class jobs existed before industrialisation? Why were they small in number?*

2 *Why did industrialisation increase the numbers of middle-class people and their influence?*

3 *Look back at what you learnt about the Industrial Revolution. How was spending in a middle-class family different from that in a working-class family?*

Where did the middle classes live?

The 19th century middle classes knew where they wanted to live – not with the working classes. Moving away from the smell and squalor of the cities was a priority for the factory owners, industrialists, professionals and clerks. And they had the money to do it. Instead of the inner city, where the Industrial Revolution had led to poverty, epidemics and misery, the middle classes moved to new residential areas on the edges of the cities, called suburbs.

The development of the railway played a key role in the creation of the new suburbs, as people did not have to live near their jobs. They could now travel to work. In London, for example, the area of North Kensington was open farmland in 1837. Sixty years later, virtually all of it was built on, with estates like the Ladbroke estate, Notting Hill that you can see in the picture.

The Ladbroke Estate, Notting Hill, London

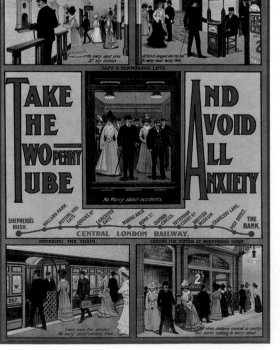

The growth of railways from the 1830s onwards meant that the wealthier middle classes could live in the suburbs and travel to work in the cities. Most middle-class suburbs developed to the west or south of the industrial cities, so that the winds wouldn't blow the whiff of the working class and the factories in their direction.

'Take the Twopenny tube.' *A poster advertising the new underground railway line, which ran between Bank and Shepherd's Bush. This was the first electric underground train line, and was opened at the beginning of the 20th century.*

66

A villa   *A semi-detached villa*   *A terraced house*

In the new suburbs, how much you earned determined the size of house you could afford to rent or, if you were very wealthy, to buy. The most expensive type of house was a villa in its own grounds. Next came semi-detached villas, and finally terraced houses. Flats were not fashionable until the 1870s.

The growth of the suburbs in London during the 19th century

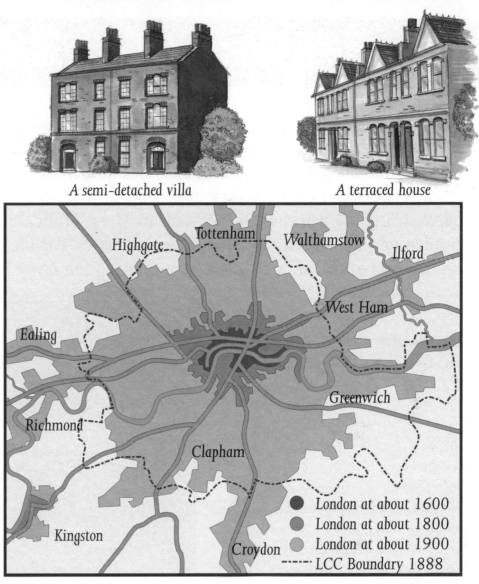

Highgate · Tottenham · Walthamstow · Ilford
Ealing · West Ham · Greenwich · Richmond · Clapham · Kingston · Croydon

● London at about 1600
● London at about 1800
● London at about 1900
----- LCC Boundary 1888

So, the middle classes lived in different sorts of houses according to what they could afford. Most could keep a servant, even if not full-time, which added to their status – their position as a member of the middle class.

1 Look back at your work on living conditions during the Industrial Revolution. What were the main differences between middle-class housing and working-class housing? Use a table like the one below to help you decide.

Similarities	Differences

2 What evidence can you find in your area of 19th century housing built for the middle classes?

3 Imagine you were living in North Kensington in 1837. What changes would you have seen? Were they good for everyone?

The middle classes had more money than the working classes, and the fun they had reflected this extra income. Whilst the working classes saw football matches, the middle classes joined golf clubs, and played tennis. In the cities, the middle classes spent time at the theatre or going to the opera, while the working classes went to Music Halls. In London, Covent Garden and Drury Lane became famous theatres. For the middle-classes, the coming of the railways also meant having fun away from home ... at the seaside.

Beside the seaside: Southport

The new railway system, which spread throughout Britain, made it possible for the middle classes to travel long distances. One of the places that developed as a result was Southport. Southport is a seaside town on the north-west coast of England in between Preston and Liverpool. In the 19th century it developed into a seaside resort visited by the middle classes. This is its story ...

Southport in the early 1800s

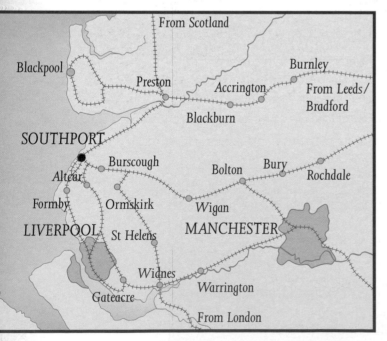

The new rail links to Southport in the 1880s

In 1801 only 300 houses stood in Southport, and the population was 2,500. The growth of the village was very gradual because it didn't have good transport links with other places. The only transport available in the early 19th century was a carriage service between local hotels and the Leeds and Liverpool Canal. Those who could afford to, used the carriage but the road was poor and the journey uncomfortable. But, with the coming of the railways, Southport changed.

By 1850 Southport was linked to the railway network and by the 1880s it was connected to Liverpool, Manchester, Preston and Scotland. Southport had three stations: Chapel Street, Lord Street and Central Station. In 1801 the population of this seaside community was 2,500; one hundred years later it was just over 64,000.

What was there to do in Southport for the middle classes?

The railway connections made it much easier for people to travel to Southport. A number of attractions were developed to bring people into the seaside resort and encourage them to stay for a holiday. There was a pier, a promenade and swimming baths. The Winter Gardens was an entertainment complex, where you could listen to music and see concerts and performances. A huge boating lake provided entertainment for those who enjoyed water. Away from the town centre, large parks were laid out so people could stroll and take in the sea air.

Bathing at Southport at the turn of the century

The middle classes were spoilt for choice when it came to accommodation. Hundreds of hotels and boarding houses were opened. The healthy sea air attracted many retired people, and the beach was the ideal setting for family fun activities.

Early holidaymakers enjoying donkey rides on Southport beach in the early 1900s

The Pier at Southport with the Victoria Hotel in the background, 1872

1 Using the map of the railway connections to Southport and the pictures of the town, plan a weekend break to the seaside:

◆ Imagine you are a clerk in a cotton mill in Manchester who has never been out of the city. You and your family plan to stay on Saturday night at a hotel near the seafront.

◆ Write a postcard home to your friend describing your route from Manchester to Southport by rail.

◆ Describe the activities you enjoyed during your weekend and explain why you decided to go to the seaside for your break.

Middle-class life in the 19th century has been represented in many different ways, for example, through paintings, television and novels. Just how accurate are these representations? Are any representations closer to history than others? Before deciding, you need to understand a bit more about middle-class life.

You already know that the term 'middle class' covers a wide range of people, jobs and incomes. This Fact File includes some other details of middle-class living.

FACT FILE

♦ The average middle-class family spent just under half of its income on food.

♦ By 1900 shops sold a wide range of foods that a middle-class family might want to buy. These included: pineapples, bananas, tinned food, custard powder, breakfast cereals and cheap meat imported from Australia and the USA.

A Victorian advert for Bird's custard powder

♦ Most middle-class families had one or more servants, such as maids and cooks. However, office workers could only pay for occasional daily help. If you were very rich, you could afford a personal carriage to take you about town and beyond.

♦ The moral values of the average middle-class family included:
  ♦ hard work for a fair wage,
  ♦ living without relying on the government for help,
  ♦ spending money carefully.

Now that you have read the fact file, you are going to look at how painters and, more recently, television have represented middle-class life.

'Home Sweet Home', painted by Walter Dendy

'Many Happy Returns of the Day', painted by William Powell

Pictures painted in the past can tell us a lot about the period but they can also tell us about what the artist wanted to show…

1 If all other evidence from the time was destroyed, what impression would you get from the paintings, of:
   ◆ 19th century middle-class families?
   ◆ How the middle class spent their money?

2 Do these impressions seem accurate when you compare them with what you have learnt and the information in the 'Fact File'?

On their own, individual paintings can be of limited value. They only show us what the artist wanted the painting to show. However, used with other sources, paintings can be more valuable. We can also decide which painting is the most accurate, by comparing them to other evidence.

...Can we rely on visual images as historical evidence?

In 1999, a television series called *The 1900 House* was broadcast by Channel 4. The Bowler family lived in a house as if the year was 1900. Everything in the house, including the clothes and food, was the same as it would have been in 1900.

The Bowler family posing for a typical Victorian family photograph

The father serves soup as the family eat lunch

3 If all other evidence from the time was destroyed, what impression would you get from the stills, of:

 ◆ 19th century middle-class families?

 ◆ How the middle class spent their money?

4 Do these impressions seem accurate when you compare them with what you have learnt and the information in the fact file?

5 The Bowler Family found it hard to live 'in 1900', yet they had the correct clothes, food and domestic servants. Does this mean the series was not accurate?

6 Look at the paintings of middle-class homes and the stills from *The 1900 House*. What are the similarities and differences between them? Use a table like the one below to help you.

Similarities	Differences

7 The paintings were completed during the 19th century but *The 1900 House* was filmed nearly a hundred years afterwards. Does this mean that the paintings give a more accurate impression of middle-class life?

As you have seen, both the paintings and the films give us some historical evidence. However, when you compare these with what you have learnt, it becomes clear that these visual images do not give us the full story. As a result, you would have to be very careful about using these as historical sources by themselves. Instead, you would have to consider all types of evidence together to get a fuller picture of what happened in the past.

8 The middle classes became very important during the 19th century. Look back at the previous spreads and write a dialogue between two members of the middle class, celebrating what they have achieved both for Britain and for their own families. Towards the end of the script introduce a member of the working class who challenges their views.

We are used to discussing issues about equality today, we think of it as normal. Millions of British men and women over the age of 18 have the right to vote in elections. They vote for the person they want to see become Member of Parliament (MP) for their area. Only people in the House of Lords, those in prison or people whom it is compulsory to hold for treatment for mental illness, are denied the right to vote.

In the 18th and 19th centuries, however, the right to vote was not thought of as normal. 200 years ago only 5% of the population could vote. Men and women viewed themselves and the opposite sex very differently to the way they do today, and equality was not an issue most people ever thought of. But, during the period 1750–1900, attitudes began to change. New ideas about the role of women reshaped beliefs. Both men and women were involved in different campaigns to change laws that discriminated against women and some men. The most important of these laws was the Franchise – the right to vote. In this section you are going to investigate why it took women so much longer than men to gain the right to vote, and why 1918 was the year they could finally vote.

In 1831 lots of things about elections were unfair, but they had been unfair for hundreds of years since Parliament began in the 13th century. So, who could vote in 1831?

Who could vote?

I can vote because I own land. It is right that only a few people have the vote. As landowners we know what's right for the country.

I practise law in the city of London. I own some land in the country and a house in the city. This gives me the right to vote.

Clergyman

I live and work in a borough. Although I don't own much property it is enough to give me the vote.

Landowner

Lawyer

Who couldn't vote?

I won my freedom from slavery a few years ago but I still can't vote, let alone stand as a candidate. I have lived in the city of Leeds for many years, but I just don't have any property.

My husband can vote, but, as a woman, I can't. He says he wants to be an MP because he owns land. All my property became his on our wedding day.

My factories in Manchester are making Britain a very wealthy country. Yet I do not have the right to vote. There are more and more factory owners – we should all have a voice in Parliament!

Whilst most of the village went off to the big city to find work in the factories a few families stayed behind. We work on the land but own none of it. We can rent some land to grow our own food but this doesn't give us the right to vote.

Shop-keeper

Rich woman   Factory owner

Farm labourer

The right to vote depended very much on where you lived. There was no nation-wide system. This led to lots of differences.

In the **county constituencies** [the rural areas] the only men who could vote were the rich property owners. In the **borough constituencies** [the urban areas] the right to vote varied. In some boroughs some tenants enjoyed the franchise and in others businessmen, clergy, professionals and tradesmen might qualify for the vote. To become an MP you had to own a lot of property. On some points however, the system was consistent – only men aged 21 or over could vote, and no woman was allowed to vote.

1 What are the key differences between those who had the right to vote in 1831 and those who didn't? Make a list of all the differences.

2 Why did rich people in 1831 think this system was fair?

Only 5% of the adult population had the vote in 1831 and these were all men. To understand why so few men had the vote we need to understand the very different attitudes and beliefs that were held at the time.

Just across the English Channel in France, new ideas about how society should be run and what rights people should have were challenging the French political system. Liberty, equality and fraternity was the slogan of the French revolutionaries in 1789. The French Revolution happened partly because of poverty and hunger similar to the poverty Britain was facing. Authorities in Britain were horrified when the French revolutionaries cut off their king's head. At a similar time, in America, the 13 English colonies had fought for and won their independence from Britain in 1783. The slogan of the revolutionaries in America was 'no taxation without representation'. This meant that, if people were to be taxed by the government, they should have the right to be represented in Parliament. Can you imagine the fear of those who ruled Britain alongside the monarch, King George III, in this period?

Landowner

BELIEF 1

I own a big house with large grounds, and rent out both to make money. Owning property is so important in giving British society order and stability. Look what happened in France during their revolution in 1789! The whole country was in chaos because the lower classes thought that they could take the property of the upper classes and govern France better. What a mess they made of it. I don't want to see Britain end up like that. I know that parliament doesn't represent everyone, but why should it? Not everyone owns property. Only those people who do own property know what a responsibility it is. That is why people from the upper class become Members of Parliament. They know what is best for everybody, so they govern on behalf of the whole country.

BELIEF 2

I don't know why some people are making a fuss about changing the voting system. It's been the same for hundreds of years. People like me aren't really interested anyway. We would rather just get on with our lives. What the MPs get up to doesn't really affect me as a labourer. They'll rule the way they always have done – for themselves! I know my place in society. I don't own property and never will. What's the point of having the vote? As long as I can fill my stomach with food at the end of the day, I don't worry.

Farm labourer

Bishop

BELIEF 3

Our voting system does not need changing. It is God's wish that society be divided into classes of people of different rank and property. The upper class knows how to rule, they have been doing it for hundreds of years. There is nothing wrong with owning property and making money. The Old Testament is full of stories of what happens when the stability of society is upset by people wanting to change things. God rules the church just like the upper classes rule Britain. It's all part of the natural order of things. Trying to change this will only end in disaster. The working class can't rule themselves. Remember what happened when Oliver Cromwell ruled? What a mess that was! They work hard and know that they have a place in heaven when they die.

The execution of Marie Antoinette during the French Revolution. In 1792, the revolutionaries murdered 1,400 landowners, priests and members of the monarchy in Paris.

1 Look at the picture of a scene from the French Revolution. Imagine you are one of the revolutionaries in the crowd. What would you be feeling? What would you be able to see and smell?

2 What can you see that would make the landowner and the bishop so afraid of change?

3 Most factory owners and businessmen did not have the vote in 1831, yet they were creating wealth by selling goods at home and abroad. In pairs, design a poster which opposes the views put by the landowner and the bishop. Include on your poster these key words:

◆ Justice   ◆ Order   ◆ Greed
◆ Power   ◆ Govern   ◆ Conditions

Why did women not have the vote in 1831?

In 1831, no women could vote. For some women gaining the vote was not important at all. Many had no interest in politics – making laws was the responsibility of men, they thought. Opportunities in education and employment improved for women during the 19th century and they had been given a number of social and economic rights as well. However, a minority was not satisfied. They thought that women's position in society would only change when women had the right to elect Members of Parliament who would secure improvements by passing new laws.

Before we look at these people and some of the improvements that took place, we need to understand women's position in society and attitudes towards women. It is 1890. This is Eliza. Eliza is going to tell you what it has been like to be a woman in the 19th century.

People think that men and women have different roles. When I was a girl, Mother taught us that women should always be obedient to their husbands and brothers. Our job is to look after them, and they go out to work. Father said that independence is a foolish thing for women to want. Women are best suited to staying at home.

Everybody said that women and men are different – men are strong and women are weak, men are more intelligent and women are too emotional. So, it made sense that men should go out into public life to work and make the decisions for us. That's why only men are MPs. Women are supposed to be better suited to the private world – staying at home and raising children. That's why they call us the 'Angel in the House'.

These views are the ideal of how women should behave, but there are women who do work of course. The poorer, working class women really. They work mostly as cooks or maids so that well-off women can run the house. Some women even do physical labour like working in mines. They are really very poor and have to help their husbands, despite the way society thinks women should behave.

The laws (made by men) support these ideas. Up until just eight years ago in 1882, a married woman was her husband's property by law. Until 1870, a wife could not own property and when she married, all her goods were owned by her husband. Even if she worked, the wages she earned belonged to her husband. There are men that treat their wives as slaves. Apparently, over the last 100 years, 300 women have been sold by their husbands! I remember in 1837 I read in the local newspaper about one wife who was taken to Walsall market to be sold. I still have the article here.

Walsall Herald

Man sells his wife!

They came into the market between ten and eleven o'clock in the morning, the woman being led by a halter, which was fastened round her neck and the middle of her body. After a few minutes she was sold to Thomas Snape; the purchase price was 2s and 6d [12.5 pence] and all seemed satisfied with the bargain.

The Church also teaches people about men and women's roles. Most people go to church. The Bible teaches that God created woman from man, and that wives should obey their husbands. The Church says that **monogamy** [having one wife or husband] and being faithful is very important. People think that the order of society depends upon the stability of the family, so the behaviour of women must be controlled. Women have always been discouraged from trying to change their situation, particularly by the Church.

This sounds very gloomy but it isn't all bad. In many cases, just to make a living and stay alive, husbands and wives have to work side by side as equals. In 1859, Charles Darwin's Origin of the Species was published. Darwin questioned the Church's attitudes and the Bible with the scientific evidence he had collected for evolution. He said women and men evolved from apes and not in the Garden of Eden. Things have changed a bit since I was a girl – we have a few more rights now. In 1857, the Divorce Act made it a bit easier for women to get divorced and education is improving too. In 1865, Elizabeth Garrett Anderson became the first female doctor. I wonder what will happen over the next few years …

1 Collect together some images of women today going about their daily lives. Compare them with the pictures you can see here. You might look for pictures of women:

◆ at work ◆ in their leisure time ◆ gaining qualfications

2 How do they compare? What do today's pictures tell you about women's roles?

In America and France, revolutionaries were demanding more political freedom and equality. In this tense and suspicious atmosphere, the government was so frightened that it was prepared to go to any lengths to stop the same thing happening in Britain. There was also much starvation and poverty all over Britain and people were unhappy. One example of the government trying to stop protest is the Pentrich Rising of 1817. It took place in Derbyshire, where a group of stocking-knitters took up *arms* [weapons] in protest, in the mistaken belief that they were part of a much bigger uprising.

Is this the story of government dirty tricks?

The stocking-knitters were caught. 35 of them were tried for treason, 23 were sentenced to death but only three were eventually hanged and beheaded – Jeremiah Brandreth, William Turner and Isaac Ludlam. The rest were transported to Australia for life. You are going to decide whether the government deliberately deceived these men and led them to believe they were part of a large uprising. Did they use a secret agent to fool the stocking-knitters?

Between March and May 1817, a man called Oliver, who people later believed was a government informer, toured the northern industrial region posing as a reformer. He made contact with many reformers and told them that hundreds of people were planning a revolt. Some poor and unemployed workers led by the stocking-knitter, Jeremiah Brandreth, believed him.

One of the executioners holdi[ng]
Jeremiah Brandreth's head

Following Oliver's plan

1 On 8 June, Brandreth met other like-minded men in Pentrich. He explained the plan to collect arms and men from surrounding villages and march to Nottingham. They would join other groups whom, he was told, were part of a large uprising. London was to be taken over and a **provisional** [temporary] government put in place.

2 On 9 June, Brandreth and his supporters visited houses and farms demanding weapons and men. They soon had between 200 and 300 men and headed for Nottingham.

What was really happening

1 Oliver told many reformers in the north that a revolt was planned all over the country. Brandreth believed him and Oliver told him the plan. Oliver then told the government in London that there was a revolution being planned.

2 When Brandreth and his men arrived in Nottingham, the thousands of men Oliver had told them about were not there. Instead, they were met by soldiers who were ready to stop the rebels. Brandreth's men fled.

1 Jeremiah Brandreth, William Turner and Isaac Ludlum were caught and put in chains. They were executed on 7 November, 1817. Is their blood on the hands of the government? Have a look at these sources and then decide, on the basis of the evidence, whether Oliver was a government informer who stirred up passion and fooled the stocking-knitters.

The government employed Oliver without knowing anything about his character. When Brandreth and the others were on trial, the government knew enough about Oliver to make them suspect that these foolish stocking-knitters had been duped [fooled] into their ridiculous uprising by him.

Historians J.L. and B. Hammond, 1919

Throughout the spring of 1817 the spy, Oliver, was going about the industrial areas posing as a delegate from one of the London reform groups. In most areas, Oliver had no success in provoking the reformers to take up arms; but in Derbyshire, where the stocking-knitters were even nearer starvation than the rest of the textile workers, Jeremiah Brandreth believed what Oliver said.

Adapted from historians GDH Cole and Raymond Postgate, 1938

The Pentrich Rising was either arranged by the Home Secretary or for him. Brandreth was not like a real revolutionary and his rebellion was useless. He didn't speak about suffrage at all. Instead, he argued for food and money for all men. Brandreth said he wanted to set up a provisional government but when he was asked what this meant, he said it was a government which gave people **provisions** [food and drink].

Adapted from historian R.J. White's beliefs about Jeremiah Brandreth

2 Looking at the evidence, do you think the government played 'dirty tricks' on the stocking-knitters?

Yes – evidence	No – evidence

3 If the government did decieve the stocking-knitters, what do you think their reasons were?

Crushing the reformers: the Peterloo Massacre

For hundreds of years people had protested against changes affecting their lives. However, the effects of industrialisation brought so much upheaval that many protested for change and not against it. Some of the *reformers* [the people who wanted change] were middle class, but had no way of getting laws changed because they had no vote. Strong forces were pressing in on the government to change the political system, to include representation for all men.

The Peterloo Massacre

On 16 August 1819, a meeting took place in St Peter's Field, Manchester. A large number of people assembled to hear Henry Hunt and other reformers talk about parliamentary reform. Unemployment was widespread and poverty was a real problem. The local magistrates were worried – what would happen next? They decided to arrest Henry Hunt before he started to speak. But, the crowd closed in around the police and armed soldiers, and they were trapped. A second group of soldiers was sent in and the crowd panicked. The soldiers also panicked and beat back the crowds with their swords…

By the end of the day 11 people lay dead and over 400 were injured. Four of the injured died soon after. This picture shows what happened that day, but remember that this is only the artist's view.

1 Draw a small picture of the face of your partner, while they do the same for you. Then, put your 'faces' on two of the people in the picture. What can you see, hear, and smell as one of the people involved at St Peter's Field. Why were you there?

2 What did the artist want people to know about the events?

What happened?

Often, we come across evidence that does not agree with other versions of the same event. This is always likely to happen because of different people's view points. To find out what happened in Manchester you must look at all the evidence.

From the windows of Mr Baxter's house ... I saw the main group proceeding towards St Peter's Field and I never saw a happier crowd ... if the men had intended mischief they would not have brought their wives, their sisters or their children with them.

Archibald Prentice, a supporter of reform

The cavalry, waving their sabres over their heads, dashed forward and began cutting people... women and youths were sabred or trampled. In ten minutes it was all over, the field was almost deserted. Several mounds of human beings still remained where they had fallen, crushed down and smothered. Some of these were still groaning, others with staring eyes.

Samuel Bamford, who had been involved in the preparations for the rally

I saw the soldiers — they were powerless and hemmed in by the crowd. Our men, the Hussars, tried to drive the people back with the flat edge of our swords. But, sometimes the blade was used instead (which can accidentally happen in these situations). The fact that more people were not hurt shows how humanely the soldiers behaved. More people were hurt from the pushing of the crowd than by our men.

Lieutenant William Joliffe of the 15th Hussars regiment, 1847

A list of those who died at the fields or soon after

Name	Cause of Death	Name	Cause of Death
Joseph Ashworth	shot	William Fildes	trampled
Thomas Ashworth*	sabred and trampled	Mary Heys	trampled
John Ashton	sabred and trampled	Sarah Jones	not recorded
William Bradshaw	not recorded	John Lees	sabred
Thomas Buckley	sabred and trampled	Arthur O'Neill	trampled
James Crompton	trampled	Martha Partington	trampled
William Dawson	sabred and trampled	John Rhodes	not recorded
Edmund Dawson	sabred		

*one of the special constables

1 Use all the sources together to write an account that is supported by the evidence, and which you believe is accurate and fair.

2 Were the events at St Peter's Fields important? If so, why?

3 What were the motives of the people there?

The effects of Peterloo

The attack on unarmed people at a public meeting, shocked many and the events in Manchester were soon being called the Peterloo Massacre, a reference to the battle of Waterloo in 1815. The government supported the magistrates who had sent in the troops and Henry Hunt was put in prison for two years. To squash any more attempts at lobbying for reform the government passed the Six Acts of 1819. These acts gave magistrates the power to search houses for weapons, only allowed political meetings with the permission of the magistrate and made it easier to bring people to trial and stop the publication of papers that might stir up people's demands for change.

In 1832, some of the campaigning that was happening around Britain paid off. Parliament passed a law which gave over 200,000 middle-class men the vote for the first time, and some of the growing industrial towns had MPs for the first time. But, women weren't included and neither were working-class men. The working class was furious and immediately pressed harder for the right to vote.

Were the Chartists actions a failure or a success?

In 1836, William Lovett, the leader of the London Working Men's Association, drew up a list of six demands to give working people a share of political power. These six demands became known as the People's Charter, and its supporters were the Chartists.

Chartists hoped that these six changes would give working-class men enough political power to make the reforms they wanted happen. A seventh point, giving women the vote, was rejected by the London Working Men's Association. The Chartist movement was about working-class men, not women.

From the start, leadership of the movement was split. William Lovett and Thomas Attwood wanted to persuade Parliament using peaceful methods. Feargus O'Connor, on the other hand, favoured force, using strikes, threats, violence and even revolution.

The People's Charter

- *The vote for every man over 21*

- *Secret voting*

- *No property qualification for MPs so that poor people can stand as candidates in elections*

- *Members of Parliament should be paid for their work*

- *All constituencies to have the same number of voters in them*

- *Annual elections*

Parliament will never take any notice of you, O'Connor. The government will only meet force with force. At least with my petition to back up the six points there is a chance they will listen. After all, one and a quarter million people have signed it!

You fool, Lovett! Don't you understand it is better to die free men than live as slaves? Physical force is treason when it fails, but it is glorious when it succeeds. Only when the government is faced with force will it give in to our six points!

◆ May 1839: the House of Commons reject the first Chartist petition. A general strike was discussed in some Chartist meetings, but came to nothing.

◆ November 1839: local Chartist leaders were imprisoned in South Wales. The attempt to free them was called the Newport Rising. When the group of Chartists stormed the hotel where the prisoners were being kept, they were met with a volley of shots that left fourteen dead.

◆ 1842: a second petition was presented to Parliament with over three million signatures on it. The House of Commons rejected it.

◆ 1848: a third petition was presented to the House of Commons. It, too, was defeated.

Soon after the last petition was defeated, the Chartist movement dissolved. Aside from the leadership disputes, the movement was only popular during hard times. When people had lost jobs they supported O'Connor and Lovett; when the economy improved and jobs became plentiful this support melted away. However, the Chartist movement did have some success because during this period many more working-class men and women realized that the vote was important to them. If they were going to make life better for themselves, they needed the vote.

The Chartist procession taking the second petition of 1842 to Parliament

1 Make a list of what you think were the strengths and weaknesses of the Chartist movement.

2 Why would some people still be unhappy with the electoral system after 1832?

3 Do you think Lovett or O'Connor's strategy would be more successful in trying to get Parliament to agree to the six points? Why?

4 Apart from having the right to vote, what other features make up a democracy?

The 1867 and 1884 Reform Acts

The 1832 Reform Act gave representation to the new industrial cities like Leeds and Manchester. It also widened the franchise by adding over 200,000 male middle-class voters to the electoral register. In 1867, the franchise was widened still further ...

In 1867, Parliament passed a second reform act which doubled the electorate by giving the right to vote to more wealthy, male urban workers and some tenant farmers.

1 *What do these pie charts and data tell you about the changes made by the 1832 and 1867 Reform Acts?*

■ *Men able to vote as a percentage of adult population.*
□ *Men unable to vote*
■ *Women (all unable to vote)*

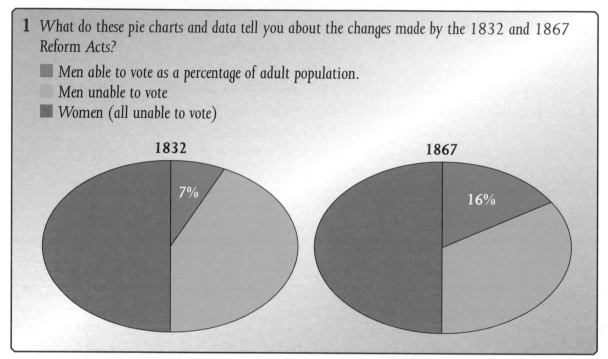

1832 — 7%   1867 — 16%

Although you can see how more men were given the vote in 1867, women were still not enfranchised. This time the issue was at least debated in Parliament, but the proposal was rejected. Aside from the increased number of voters, the growing cities and large towns now had representation through Members of Parliament.

Why was the franchise extended?

After the 1832 reform the government hoped that pressures for even more change would subside and the upper classes would continue to hold power in Parliament. But this wasn't to be. The Chartists campaign was not immediately successful, but it did keep the issue alive in the press and in the minds of MPs. The large numbers of workers in the new industrial cities were also becoming better informed because of the improvements in communications. As a result, the working class found it easier to co-ordinate activities in support of demands for political change. Extending the franchise was bound to come sooner or later.

2 *Why do you think the number of men enfranchised increased so slowly after 1832?*

In 1884, the Third Reform Act was passed by Parliament. It more than doubled the number of voters by extending the vote to many male agricultural and urban workers, including some tenants. Not only did it increase the percentage of men able to vote, it also divided the country up into **constituencies** [areas] with a single MP to represent each one.

3 Now, look at the pie chart showing the *1884 Reform Act*.

◆ Which of the three reform acts was the most important in terms of the franchise?

◆ Why would some working-class people still not be satisfied with the results of these reforms?

■ Men able to vote as a percentage of adult population.

■ Men unable to vote

■ Women (all unable to vote)

1884

29%

Looking back over the past fifty-odd years we've seen a lot of changes. More and more people can vote, which has satisfied all those making a fuss about change. Of course, women still can't vote and that's right and proper given their silly minds and their tendency to get emotional. Thankfully, MPs are still not paid for being politicians. This means that only the rich can afford to stand for election to Parliament, so I am pleased to tell you that they share similar attitudes to myself about who should really govern the country and make the laws.

4 Did any of the reform acts benefit women? Explain your answer.

5 Did the reform acts of 1832, 1867 and 1884 turn Britain into a democracy as we know it today?

Men's attitudes towards women and women's attitudes towards themselves began to change after 1850 — but slowly. It took a long time for traditional attitudes to break down and for new ideas about women and their role in society to take their place. How did this happen?

Before 1850, most women were limited by male attitudes of what they could and couldn't do. Look at these pictures of this middle-class woman. She was trapped in a cycle from which there was no escape!

A number of developments took place in the 19th century, which all played their part in changing attitudes. Most of these came about because of industrialisation.

Women stay at home and look after the family.

Women don't need an education or qualifications.

If they work — women don't get good jobs.

Employment

During the 19th century the population increased and so did the number of schools. From 1870, attendance at school became compulsory, so the demand for teachers soared. By 1900, three quarters of all teachers were women. In spite of this development, if female teachers got married they had to leave school because they now had a husband who would keep them.

In the 1800s many new hospitals were built and these needed nurses. In 1860, St Thomas' Hospital in London started to train nurses. By 1900 there were 60,000 trained nurses. But, as with teaching, once nurses were married they had to resign.

In 1800, clerical jobs like keeping accounts and secretarial work were filled by men. However, the invention of the typewriter in 1868 resulted in female clerks replacing males because they could be paid less. Again, as with teaching and nursing, marriage meant you had to leave.

Early telephone exchanges from the 1880s could only work with a lot of people and nearly all were women.

Women operating an early telephone exchange

Education

London University allowed women to become students for the first time in 1848.

The first female colleges at Cambridge University were founded in 1871 and 1872.

Elizabeth Garrett Anderson became the first woman to qualify as a doctor in 1865.

1 Look back at what you have learnt about the role of women. Draw up two lists. In the first list, write those attitudes towards women that seem to be changing after 1850 and in the second, those attitudes that are the same as before.

2 Why would improved opportunities for women at school and in university affect their job prospects?

3 What other changes would need to take place if women were to have the same rights as men?

4 Compare the jobs that women could do in the 19th century, with the jobs that most women would do before industrialisation. What factors caused the changes? Think about the links between factors like: technology, urbanisation, population increase, demands for an educated workforce.

Two women who tried to make a difference

Not all women conformed to the 'ideal' image of women. Some wanted to make changes and had a hard struggle in the 19th century. They could not work through trade unions because men didn't want them as members, so some women decided to go it alone. They had to rely on their own resources and their own determination. This is the story of two women who did just that, and made a difference.

As you read about the work of these two women reformers consider these questions:

1 *Which groups of women did each reformer try to help?*

2 *Which reformer was the more successful?*

3 *Why was it that men didn't lead these campaigns for reform rather than women?*

4 *Are methods used by reformers today any different?*

Josephine Butler

Josephine Butler helped prostitutes. Driven by her Christianity and a strong desire to stop social injustices, she began visiting the local prison. Here, she met women convicted of prostitution. In her view women had not chosen to sell their bodies, they had been forced into prostitution because of low earnings and unemployment.

Josephine Butler

One campaign she led was against the Contagious Diseases Acts of 1866 and 1869. Syphilis and gonorrhoea were very common sexually transmitted diseases and could be fatal. The laws made it possible to force a woman suspected of being a prostitute to undergo a painful examination. If she had the diseases she would be taken to a 'Lock Hospital' until cured. If she refused to be examined she faced up to three months' imprisonment. The two acts only applied to **garrison** towns [army towns] but some members of the government wanted to extend them to the whole country. Josephine Butler fought hard to change the laws – after all, women weren't the only ones to blame for the spread of the diseases.

What methods did she use? How successful was she?

Josephine made public speeches, organised petitions and produced leaflets. Over 18,000 petitions signed by over 2.5 million people were presented to Parliament between 1870 and 1886. In a by-election in Colchester, she campaigned against Sir Henry Storks, a supporter of the laws. He was defeated.

Josephine established the Anti-Contagious Diseases Acts Association, which had a weekly paper called The Shield. But, there was considerable opposition to her campaign. Many found it shocking to hear and read about sexual matters in public. In the face of considerable opposition, Josephine managed to prevent Parliament extending the Acts to the whole country. Eventually, in 1886, the Acts were overturned.

Caroline Norton

Caroline Norton helped women who were trapped in unhappy marriages. Caroline was herself married to a violent man. George Norton hit her on several occasions. Caroline found out that the laws treated wives as if they didn't exist – they were non-persons. In 1836 her husband took her to court, accusing her of adultery. Although he lost the case, George Norton left her soon afterwards and took everything. He took Caroline's three children, her possessions and even the royalties she earned from the novels she had written – all, by law, were his.

Caroline Norton

For a woman, getting a divorce was very hard indeed. It was a slow and expensive process and you had to prove cruelty, bigamy or incest. Only four women had successfully divorced their husbands in the previous 200 years. Caroline's personal trauma spurred her on, and the obvious injustice of her case gained her many friends. Over the next thirty years she worked to get a fair deal for herself, her children and other wives made powerless by the laws that favoured husbands.

What methods did she use? How successful was she?

Caroline was, in some senses, lucky. She was a good writer and had contacts with important people. She wrote pamphlets and letters. She even wrote to Queen Victoria about her plight:

I pray Your Majesty knows about the effect of the married woman's non-existence in law. My husband has a right to everything and I have no claim on him.

More and more women and men joined her campaign. In 1839 she enjoyed success. The Custody of Infants Act gave divorced mothers legal custody of children under seven, and access to older children up to the age of 16.

Changes to the law on divorce had to wait until the 1857 Matrimonial Causes Act. This altered the way the law was put into practice. For example, instead of having to go before Parliament, cases would come before a special court. Women could bring divorce cases on grounds of cruelty and desertion. The Act also stated that divorced women were seen as widows and therefore had rights over their own property.

The 1857 Act still didn't make women equal with men however. Adultery was enough of a reason for a husband to divorce his wife, but not a good enough reason for a wife to divorce her husband. This sort of discrimination shouldn't surprise you. Very few women or men were thinking in terms of equality in the middle of the 19th century. Even by 1900 only 582 people had obtained a divorce under the 1857 Act. It wasn't until 1923 that men and women had similar divorce rights.

Arguments for and against female suffrage

It would be a mistake to think that the **enfranchisement** of women [giving women the vote] was bound to happen sooner or later. There were plenty of women as well as men who fought furiously to stop MPs from giving women the right to vote.

What were the arguments against giving women the right to vote?

More people were against women having the vote than in favour of it. In the early years of the Suffrage movement many treated it as a joke, and plenty of women opposed the campaign .

> **1** Read these arguments against female suffrage put forward at the time. Decide which one would would have been put forward by each of the following people:
>
> ◆ a male MP ◆ an upper-class mother ◆ a priest
>
> **2** Explain your choices.

1 *Some scientists claim to have 'proved' that women's brains are smaller than men's. This means they are less intelligent and more emotional. They cannot be trusted with the vote or the power they would enjoy if they took over Parliament.*

2 *It was God's idea that men should rule over women. In the Bible it says that Eve was formed from the rib of Adam and so she must obey him.*

3 *Women have no need of the vote because men represent women's views in parliament. Men's roles are to feed and protect their families and to run the government. The role of women is to run the home and bring up children. Male MPs are husbands and fathers and so they understand women's interests and concerns.*

Male MP

Upper-class mother

Priest

What were the arguments in favour of giving women the right to vote?

The small number of women and smaller number of men who campaigned for the right for women to vote, voiced a lot of arguments to support their case.

3 Read these arguments put forward at the time in favour of female suffrage. Which would have been put forward by each of the following people:

◆ a female doctor,   ◆ a male MP in the Labour Party,   ◆ a working-class mother.

4 Explain your choices.

1 *The vote would allow women to protect themselves and others in Britain against bad laws. It would remove obstacles in the way of a fair day's wage for a fair day's work. Granting women the right to vote would lead to an improvement in pay, conditions and the life of working-class women.*

2 *Women should be given the vote on the grounds of individual human rights and equality before the law. The vote would complement the gains in education and employment. Women have made remarkable progress during the 19th century. It is time the political system recognised this and included women in the development of democracy.*

3 *Women have had a lot of experience in local democracy. The **Antis** [those against female suffrage] argue that women would disrupt elections, become obsessed with politics and neglect their families. But in the Conservative, Liberal and Labour Parties there are women's groups who help at election time. In New Zealand women were given the vote in 1893 without any negative effects.*

Female doctor   Male Labour MP   Working-class mother

5 Pick out words from each view which *show support* for women's suffrange, and words which *show disapproval*.

6 Which of the arguments in favour of giving women the right to vote contains evidence which could be used to discredit the arguments of the **Antis** [those against women's suffrage]?

When a group of people want a reform or change in the law they can form a *pressure group*. This is different from a political party. A pressure group is usually focused on one particular issue, whereas a political party has to have policies on a range of issues, and aims to secure power by winning elections. Pressure groups do not try to win elections. They hope to influence the public and the parties and win their support.

The Suffrage Movement was a pressure group which used peaceful means of persuasion. Since the 1860s, groups of women had been campaigning for the right to vote. Although women had made gains in areas such as education, real change could only come through having a say in Parliament.

Mostly, the women and men of the Suffrage Movement were middle class. They had the time and money to spend on the campaign, unlike working-class supporters. But in 1897 the National Union of Women's Suffrage Societies (NUWSS) was formed to bring the local organisations into one. Members were called *Suffragists* and their leader was Mrs Millicent Fawcett. If Mrs Fawcett could have given an interview on the television, what would she have said about the NUWSS?

Interviewer: Good evening Mrs Fawcett. Could you tell us about your movement's beliefs?

Mrs Fawcett: Well, we believe that winning the vote for women should be achieved using peaceful tactics. I want the NUWSS to show the world how we can achieve reforms without violence. Not like those men who blow up buildings, kill people and do other ridiculous things when they want a change to the law.

Interviewer: Tell us a bit about the way you go about trying to make a change.

Mrs Fawcett: We hold meetings to generate publicity and recruit new members. Guest speakers are invited to talk about issues concerning women. These meetings might be held in people's houses or, for larger public meetings, in places like Trafalgar Square. Bus and tram stations, village greens, factory gates and breweries are just some of the places where we have spelt out our message.

We also use demonstrations. They are very good publicity, as the events are covered by the press. We dress in the colours of the Suffrage movement to great effect – purple for dignity, white for purity and green for hope. Demonstrators also dress up in the costumes of famous women, in working clothes or in national costumes, to show women's achievements. Banners showing portraits of the leaders are carried, and bands play protest songs to keep spirits high and attract attention.

Interviewer: And what about politicians? Do you trust them?

Mrs Fawcett: MPs are a prime target for the Suffrage movement. Without the support of MPs the law cannot be changed. We have tried to influence MPs and petitioned Parliament. In 1887, seventy-one MPs formed a committee in support of our cause. The work of the committee and the NUWSS has partly paid off. Almost every year a proposal has gone before Parliament to allow female suffrage, although these have all been rejected.

Liberal MPs seemed to be the most likely to support female suffrage, so a lot of effort was put into supporting candidates who were sympathetic to the Suffragists. In Wimbledon, for example, we ran the entire Liberal election campaign in 1907. But, the Liberal government was unwilling to commit itself to female suffrage, so, in 1912 we changed allegiance to the Labour Party.

Interviewer: Do you think your methods are working?

Mrs Fawcett: In spite of all these efforts the franchise law still hasn't been extended to include women. But, I'm not concerned by the lack of progress. I believe the movement is like a glacier – it might be slow-moving but it is a powerful and unstoppable force.

By the end of the 19th century there were about 400 NUWSS branches all over Britain. In 1910 membership had grown to 21,000 and by 1914 it was 53,000.

NUWSS local branches by 1899

> 1 Imagine you are a male reporter for a newspaper in 1900. Write a report on the Suffragists and their methods of campaigning. Think about whether you agree with them and their actions or not

Some pressure groups use violence to increase publicity, gain attention and pressure governments into giving in to their demands for reform. The campaigners believe that by using illegal methods they will quicken the pace of change and avoid a long drawn-out campaign. So, did violence help or hinder the Suffrage movement?

Some women lost patience with the peaceful tactics of the NUWSS. They were not producing results. By 1900, women's suffrage had been rejected fifteen times since it was first put before Parliament in 1867. In 1903, Emmeline Pankhurst and her daughter, Christobel, formed a breakaway group called the Women's Social and Political Union (WSPU). Members were called *Suffragettes*. Whereas the NUWSS campaigned only for the vote, the WSPU also wanted better working and living conditions for women. 'Deeds not Words' was the motto of the new organisation. Imagine that Mrs Pankhurst could also give an interview today. What might she say about the WSPU?

Interviewer: Thank you for joining us, Mrs Pankhurst. Would you like to tell us about the WSPU's tactics for achieving the vote for women?

Mrs Pankhurst: We have chosen direct action to make our point. We produce clever posters, organise demonstrations, smash windows, chain ourselves to railings and set fire to postboxes. We have fought police when we were arrested, and went on hunger strike when imprisoned. Some members of the WPSU have cut telegraph wires, killed plants at Kew Gardens and ruined all-male golf courses by burning 'No Votes, No Golf' into the turf with acid.

One Suffragette, Mary Richardson, attacked a painting in the National Gallery with an axe. She has become known as 'Slasher Mary.' Mary wanted to highlight the way the public seemed to have more respect for a work of art than it did for the life of a woman (at the time, I was very weak as a result of hunger striking).

Interviewer: And have your more violent methods been successful?

Mrs Pankhurst: We may have broken the law many times over but violent action has won us massive publicity. The WSPU is particularly successful in London where thirty-four branches have sprung-up compared with fifty-four in the rest of the country. Half a million people attended our meeting in London in June 1908. We worked together with the Labour Party, who came out in favour of economic and social equality for women in 1907. But, even so, by 1914 women still did not have the right to vote.

Interviewer: Do you think you will win the vote in the end?

Mrs Pankhurst: Although we are now at war with Germany, I believe women can prove that they should be given the vote, through working to help the war effort.

1 *Which of the Suffragettes' methods helped their campaign?*

2 *Which of their methods hindered their campaign?*

3 *Which, if any, of the Suffragettes' actions would be likely to persuade MPs to support female suffrage?*

4 *Continue your newspaper report from the previous pages. What would your views on the Suffragettes be? Would you approve of their methods?*

Propaganda and the Suffrage campaign

Propaganda is one of the most important weapons a pressure group can use. Groups want people to see them in a certain way. They want everybody to know about their views and the cause they are fighting for, which they achieve through publicity. We call this Propaganda. Propaganda comes in different shapes and forms. Its content could be an outright lie, but is more likely to be a half-truth, or a truth taken out of context.

Both the NUWSS and the WSPU used propaganda. Plays, poems, short stories and articles appeared in their newspapers, such as the Women's Suffrage Journal. Soap, cakes and stock cubes sold in NUWSS and WSPU shops all had the purple, white and green Suffrage colours on them. The sales from such items made lots of money for the campaign and worked as publicity. Other new techniques included groups of women riding about town with decorated bicycles to publicise demonstrations. At the 1908 F.A. Cup Final, a kite was flown with 'Votes for Women' written on it, and at one of the Oxford and Cambridge boat races a launch was decorated with Suffragette banners.

A selection of WSPU and NUWSS items, sold in their shops

1 One of the most common forms of propaganda is the poster. Here you can see several examples of posters which accompanied the suffrage campaign. As you look at each one think about these points:

◆ How can you tell if the poster is from the Suffragettes or the Suffragists?

◆ Who is each poster aimed at?

◆ What message does the poster try to put across?

◆ How effective is the poster in presenting its message?

2 If you were designing posters for both the Suffragettes and the Suffragists how would they be different? Now, make your own poster for either the Suffragettes or the Suffragists using what you have learnt.

Dying for the cause?

Take an egg and one pint of milk. Mix them together. Now drink them through your nose…You would probably refuse to do this, but the woman in this picture couldn't say 'No'. She was force-fed the dairy mixture by prison officials acting on British government orders. Why?

Some of the women who used violence were arrested and put in prison. To protest about their detention and to attract publicity, some refused to eat or drink and went on hunger-strike. The government couldn't allow women to die of hunger in prison, so it issued orders to prison officers – 'force-feed anyone who refuses meals.' It worked. The prisoners survived, but the stories of how they were treated got out – and into newspapers and magazines. Mary Leigh, one of those force-fed, describes her experiences:

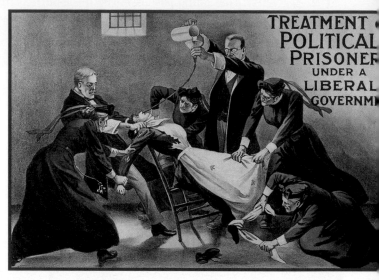

> *I was surrounded and forced back on to the chair, which was tilted backwards. While I was held down, a nasal tube was inserted. It was two yards long, with a funnel at the end. The end is put up the left and right nostril on alternate days. The sensation is most painful – the eardrums seem to be bursting and there is a horrible pain in the throat and the breast. The tube is pushed down twenty inches. The one holding the funnel pours the liquid down. The after-effects are a feeling of faintness and a great pain in the breast, nose and ears. I was sick on the first occasion.*

Over a thousand women were force-fed in this way. Although the government kept the hunger-strikers alive, the sympathetic publicity given to these women painted the government in a bad light. This was great for the Suffrage campaign, but terrible for the Prime Minister and his cabinet. What should the government do with the hunger-strikers? The government had four options:

1 Let them die.

2 Let them out of prison and re-arrest them when they were better.

3 Let them out of prison.

4 Stop arresting women who broke the law.

> 1 *What would be the good and bad points of taking each of these decisions? Think about this first from the government's point of view and then from the Suffragettes' point of view.*

Playing cat and mouse

The government chose option 2. On 25 April, 1913, Parliament passed a new law that allowed the prison authorities to release hunger-strikers to give them time to recover. The police watched them and as soon as the women were better, they were arrested again. Not surprisingly, women didn't go back to prison voluntarily. This new law got the government out of a sticky situation – no one died and the publicity surrounding the treatment of Suffragettes in prison faded from the headlines. The Suffragettes responded to this by calling the new law the Cat and Mouse Act, and used it to good effect as part of their poster campaign.

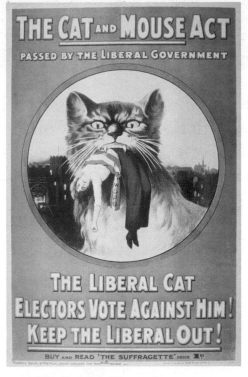

Unequal society, unequal treatment

Not all hunger-strikers were treated the same however. The level of brutal treatment seems to have depended on your class. Upper and middle-class women were treated reasonably well, working-class women were not. In 1911, Lady Constance Lytton disguised herself as a working-class woman called Jane Wharton. As her real, upper-class self, Lady Constance Lytton was imprisoned but always medically examined and found to be unfit to be force-fed. When she pretended to be Jane Wharton she was not examined and was force-fed seven times. These women were treated like all other prisoners, which was a shock to them and the public, as they were considered respectable women.

Read these historians' views on the hunger strikers.

George Dangerfield:

The Suffragettes were women who enjoyed the experience of imprisonment.

Roger Fulford:

Force-feeding was a harmless procedure that had been in use for years with 'lunatics'.

Jane Marcus:

The Suffragettes were committed activists who were prepared to give up everything to win the right to vote.

2 Which historian's view seems most justified given the evidence you have looked at so far?

3 Imagine you are in support of the government. Write a letter to the head of Holloway Prison praising the treatment of Suffragettes, and the Cat and Mouse Act. What would your opinions be? What would you think about treating Suffragettes from different social classes differently?

4 What did the government hope to gain from treating the Suffragettes in the way they did?

By the outbreak of war in 1914, the public were becoming more and more fed-up with the Suffragette's campaign of violence, and the Antis had a lot of success in disrupting the Suffragette meetings. The Cat and Mouse Act removed what had previously been a useful source of public sympathy for the Suffragettes. With each debate in Parliament, fewer and fewer MPs supported female suffrage. Between 1907 and 1914, the bill for women's enfranchisement was rejected six times.

There is a debate amongst some historians about how effective the Suffragette's violent campaign actually was. Paula Bartley, for example, believes it helped them:

> Historians have sometimes argued that the violence of the WSPU destroyed support for votes for women, because it upset the public and MPs. It also gave the Liberal government an ideal excuse to deny women the vote. But, this is not true. The long peaceful campaign before 1905 had not persuaded the House of Commons to extend the suffrage. Even in 1910, when the WSPU stopped using violence and used peaceful tactics, women were still not given the vote. So, it seems that the government and society were not willing to grant women the vote whatever methods they used to campaign.

An incident at the Derby Race of 1913. The Suffragette, Emily Davison, ran under the barriers to pin a WSPU ribbon on to the saddle of the King's horse. She got caught up under the horse and died two days later.

Others like Bob Ellis believe the opposite – that violence destroyed any chance of women gaining the vote:

> The violence of the WSPU made it difficult for the Liberal government to give women the vote. Prime Minister Asquith said the government was certainly not willing to give in to violence when it hadn't wanted to give in to **reason** [peaceful discussion]. Many women also disagreed with the violence, and it was women and not men who organised the first anti-suffrage groups.

Suffragettes' campaign for the vote?

1 Study the following sources and, using your own knowledge, decide whether you think violence helped or hindered the Suffragettes campaign. Use this table to help you.

Helped	Hindered	Both

1

Haven't the Suffragettes the sense to see that the very worst way of campaigning for the vote is to try and **intimidate** [scare] or blackmail a man into giving them what he would gladly give otherwise?

Lloyd George, Liberal MP and future Prime Minister, talking about extending the vote to women, May 1913

2

I hope that the more old-fashioned Suffragists will stand by their comrades [the Suffragettes] who I believe have done more for women's suffrage in twelve months than the NUWSS have been able to do in the same number of years.

Adapted from a letter written by Mrs Fawcett, leader of the peaceful NUWSS, when members of the WSPU were in prison

3

The argument of politicians and the Suffragists has always been that once public opinion agrees with us then, without any force at all, women will be given the vote. But, in 1906, there was a very large section of the public who were in favour of women's suffrage and what good did that do the cause? We asked the government to give us the vote but they didn't. So, now we will fight for our cause.

Adapted from 'My Own Story' by Emmeline Pankhurst, founder of the NUWSS

4

When the Suffragettes began their campaign they were mistaken for featherheads. They were not taken seriously. Now they have proved they are very serious, they have frightened the government, they have broken the law, they have made votes for women practical politics.

Adapted from a comment in the Daily Mirror, 1906

2 'If the Suffragette movement had been less **militant** [violent] and more peaceful, would women have been given the vote by 1914?' Use the sources and your own knowledge to answer this question. Write an account which explores this issue, making use of your knowledge and the evidence you have studied.

In 1914, neither the Suffragists nor the Suffragettes had been successful in winning the vote. Yet, in 1918, at the end of the war, women over 30 did gain the vote. Why was this? Did the change have anything to do with women's efforts during the war?

At the start of the First World War in August 1914, many men from Britain rushed to join the armed forces and fight with the French against Germany and her allies. With thousands of men leaving their usual jobs, women were encouraged to fill the gaps and make a contribution to the war effort. By the summer of 1915 many responded by working long hours on the land or in factories.

As soon as the war started, both the Suffragists and the Suffragettes stopped their campaigns for suffrage. They believed it was their duty to support the government in a crisis. The war might also offer opportunities for the suffrage movement to show those who disagreed with them just what women were capable of. Mrs Fawcett said in August 1914, 'Let us show ourselves worthy of citizenship.' If women could show the government that, like men, they could 'fight' to defend the Empire, maybe they also deserved to have the right to vote.

What work did women do?

Encouraged by the Government, many women stepped into men's jobs as well as the new jobs that were created by the extra need to manufacture clothing and munitions and grow food.

> **1** Do you think the following table and pictures support the view that women were 'worthy of citizenship,' as Mrs Fawcett suggested?

The main jobs of women working on the Home Front, 1914–1918

Jobs	Number of women working in 1914	Number of women working in 1918
Munitions [weapons]	212,000	947,000
Transport	18,200	117,200
Agriculture	190,000	228,000
Industry	2,180,000	2,971,000
Domestic service	1,658,000	1,250,000

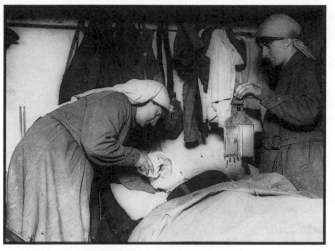

Mairi Chisholm tending to a wounded soldier in Pervyse, France, in 1917

A female gravedigger

What did men think of it all?

Women did all sorts of jobs – bus and tram conductresses, railway porters and ticket collectors, postwomen and policewomen. They swept roads, carried coal and worked in breweries. Most of these jobs were considered unsuitable for women before the war broke out. Women were also paid less than the men had been. Many of the men who did not go to fight, objected to working with women. Members of trade unions were worried that when the soldiers returned after the war they would not get their jobs back or that they would earn less money. Agreements were made between the unions and the government stating that men could have their jobs back when they returned from the war.

Men and women working together in a munitions workshop during the war

...Why did women get the vote in 1918 and not before?

> **3** Look at these two sources about male attitudes towards women during the war. What do they tell you about men's attitudes to women working for the war effort?
>
> **4** Do they show that men thought women were 'worthy of citizenship' and should be given the vote?

The men led us a devil of a life ... they cut a petrol pipe half through, they'd unscrew a valve, they would change over the leads on the spark plugs ... they'd empty oil out of your lamps ... they would give us the wrong directions.

Elizabeth Lee was a driver in the Army Service Corps. After a month's trial, and despite constant harassment, she decided to stay.

A picture from an article in the Illustrated War News, October 1917. The article was called 'Rough work but ready workers: girl "coalies"'. It was published by the government and to encourage women to work.

We have looked at women's work during the war, and what men in society thought about women's efforts. We also know that women over 30 were given the vote in 1918. But, what was the reason? Was it because of their efforts during the war or was there another reason?

In 1915, the government realised that the voting system would need changing before the next election. If the system was not reformed, thousands of soldiers would not be able to vote because they had not lived in the same place for twelve months before an election. The law had to be changed and women seized the opportunity. They put pressure on the government to include female suffrage in the new law for men. There was no violence this time. Instead, discussions took place between politicians and suffrage leaders. There were two key differences between women's efforts to gain the vote in 1914 and in 1918:

1 Herbert Asquith was no longer Prime Minister (in 1916, the job was taken by David Lloyd George).

2 By 1915, the army still needed men but industry also needed workers. As a result, more women were encouraged into work. Employers had to change their attitudes about women working, and their attitudes to women's roles.

Some historians argue that the work done by women during the First World War was the key factor in winning the right to vote in 1918. Others say that the long campaign by the Suffragists and Suffragettes finally reached its goal, helped by the new opportunity – the fact that the voting system needed to be changed. What do you think? The information on the next page will help you decide which view is more justified.

My opposition to women's right to vote is well known. However, for three years now the Suffragettes have not started that horrible campaign of violence. Not only that, they have contributed to every service during this war except that of fighting. I therefore believe that some kind of women's suffrage should be given.

Part of a speech by Herbert Asquith, 1917

A very narrow view would see the vote as a reward for loyal wartime service. Careful study shows how **little** changed from the war, not how much. In farms, hospitals and factories, working women were greatly resented. In fact, politicians said that women who had raised children successfully had performed a service for the government, instead of those women who worked. So, it seems that working during the war did not help to get women the vote.

Adapted from a history book written in 1998

ON HER
THEIR LIVES DEPEND

WOMEN MUNITION WORKERS

Enrol at once

A government poster put up during the war to encourage women to work in munitions factories

Had there been no violence from the suffragettes and no war, women would have gained the vote, although more slowly. But without the faithful preparation of the ground over many years by Millicent Fawcett and her colleagues, neither **militancy** [violence] nor the war could have achieved the vote.

Adapted from the obituary in the Guardian newspaper for Millicent Fawcett, 1929

In 1918, the vote was granted to women aged over 30 years. This can be explained partly as the result of a fifty-year campaign. During the campaign, some of the fears about women's **enfranchisement** [right to vote] had been reduced. It can also be explained as a result of the decision to change the voting system.

Adapted from a history book written in 1995

---

1 If the First World War hadn't happened, do you think women would still have got the vote in 1918?

The number of men allowed to vote was increased in 1832, 1867, 1884 and 1918. But, women over 30 were only given the right to vote in 1918 after a long struggle lasting over fifty years. Why was it that women were slower than men in gaining the franchise?

Several factors made it harder for women to secure voting rights than for men.

1 Married women were the husband's property

To get the vote the law had to be changed. To change the law an Act of Parliament had to be passed by both the House of Commons and the House of Lords.

2 Women's place is in the home

Most women were uneducated and their place was in the home. Their lives were a mix of looking after the home, bringing up children, and hard physical work for poorer women. But, after 1850, educational opportunities increased and more and more women began to question the role that they had been given by society.

3 The Church reinforced the belief in female 'inferiority'

In the book of Genesis, Eve was created from one of Adam's ribs. It was therefore natural that women should obey their husbands and keep a good home. Just as God was at the head of the Christian church, so a husband was at the head of his family.

A woman voting in a general election for the first time in 1918

4 The opposition of trade unions

Trade unions had developed during the 19th century, largely to support working-class men. Unions did not allow female members. So, while men made some gains in political, social and economic rights, women did not have a national voice to speak for them. They had to rely on very determined individuals to make a change.

5 Campaigns need money

Male political organisations, like unions, could build up funds for campaigns because of membership fees. Women, on the other hand, had no such resource to support their fight for the vote. It was only when wealthier middle-class women supported suffrage in large numbers that they could afford to pay for campaign expenses.

6 Why should women have the vote?

Many people didn't believe that giving women the vote would make Great Britain any greater. Without female suffrage, Britain had industrialised ahead of all other countries, created the largest empire the world had seen and become one of the world's richest countries. Why would giving more people the vote make things better? How could they be better?

All these factors taken together help to explain why it took women so much longer than men to achieve suffrage.

1 Take each factor in turn. Suppose it had not existed during the 19th century. Would female suffrage have happened any quicker? Which factors are more important than others?

2 Use the chart above, and what you have learnt to help you answer the question 'Why did women and some men have to struggle for the vote, and why did it take women so much longer to get the vote?'

Acknowledgements

Every effort has been made to contact the holders of copyright material but if any have been inadvertently overlooked the Publishers will be pleased to make the necessary arrangements at the first opportunity.

Photographs

The publishers would like to thank the following for permission to reproduce photographs on these pages:

T=top,B=bottom,C=centre,L=left,R=right

The Advertising Archive Ltd, 70, 101; The Art Archive/Eileen Tweedy, 42–43; Barnardos Photographic Library, 57; Beamish, The North of England Open Air Museum, County Durham, 37TL, 37TC, 37TR, 37BL, 37BC, 37BR; © Bettmann/Corbis, l9T; Bridgeman Art Library, 20CL, 22, 29C, 48; Bridgeman Art Library/Christiets Images, London, UK, 71, 73; Bridgeman Art Library/Harrogate Museums and Art Gallery, North Yorkshire, UK, 71; Bridgeman Art Library/Illustrated London News Picture Library, 78; By courtesy of the British Library, 23; By courtesy of BT Archives, 89; Channel Tunnel Group, ST; Chris Ridley Photography, London, 72; © Co–operative Union Ltd 1996, 33; Derby City Libraries, 80; Dr H. J. Foster, 68; Fotomas Index UK, 53TR; Getty Images / Imagebank, SBR; The Guildhall Library, 85; © Hulton Getty, 10TL, llT, 90, 95T, 102, 108–109; The Illustrated London News Picture Library, 105TL, 106; Imperial War Museum, 105TR (Q31237), 105B (Q30124), 107 (Q105938); © Reproduced by permission of the Ironbridge Gorge Museum Trust, Elton Collection, 32B; The Kobal Collection/Diamond Films, 59T, 59B; By courtesy of the Lancashire County Museums Service, 18T; Leeds Library and Information Services, l5T, l5C; London's Transport Museum, 66BL; Manchester Central Library, 82; Mary Evans Picture Library, 29TL, 29CR, 45T, 53BL, 78CL, 91, 97, 99TL, 99TR, 100T; Mary Evans/ The Woman's Library, 99BL, 99BR; Metropolitan Borough of Sefton Leisure Services, 69T, 69CL, 69CR; The Music Carnavalet, Paris, AKG London/Lessing, 77; The Museum of London, 96, 98B; The National Grid, SBL; National Library of Australia, 49; Peak District Mining Museum, 37TL, 37TC, 37TR; Peter Newark's Historical Pictures, 53BC; Popperfoto, 20B; © Punch Ltd, 52, 61; Rex Features Ltd, 38; The Robert Opie Collection, 38; The Royal Borough of Kensington Central Libraries and Arts Service, 66TR; The Royal Collection ~ 2002 Her Majesty Queen Elizabeth II, 58; Science and Society Picture Library, 9TR; Science and Society Picture Library/Science Museum, 18B; Science and Society Picture Library/National Railway Museum, l9B; ~ Tate, London 2002, 78TR; Timepix Ltd, 6R, 7R, 10BR, l lB; © The Board of Trustees of the Victoria & Albert Museum, 55; The Waterways Trust: British Waterways Archive, 8B.

Artwork

All Artwork by Peter Bull

Index

Index